# Table of Contents

| | |
|---|---|
| Alphabetical Order | 3–5 |
| Compound Words | 6, 7 |
| Antonyms | 8, 9 |
| Synonyms | 10, 11 |
| Homophones | 12, 13 |
| **Review** | **14** |
| Nouns | 15, 16 |
| Common Nouns | 17 |
| Proper Nouns | 18–20 |
| Common and Proper Nouns | 21 |
| Plural Nouns | 22–26 |
| **Review** | **27** |
| Possessive Nouns | 28, 29 |
| Pronouns | 30–32 |
| Possessive Pronouns | 33 |
| Abbreviations | 34 |
| Adjectives | 35, 36 |
| Adjectives and Nouns | 37 |
| Adjectives | 38 |
| Prefixes | 39 |
| Suffixes | 40 |
| **Review** | **41** |
| Verbs | 42, 43 |
| Helping Verbs | 44 |
| Past-Tense Verbs | 45 |
| Present-Tense Verbs | 46 |
| Future-Tense Verbs | 47 |
| **Review** | **48** |
| Irregular Verbs | 49–51 |
| Linking Verbs | 52 |
| **Review** | **53** |
| Adverbs | 54, 55 |
| Prepositions | 56 |
| Articles | 57 |
| Commas | 58 |
| Articles and Commas | 59 |
| Commas | 60 |
| Capitalization | 61 |

# Table of Contents

Commas .......................................................................... 62

**Review** ...................................................................... **63**

Parts of Speech .......................................................... 64–66

And and But .................................................................. 67

Subjects ........................................................................ 68

Predicates .................................................................... 69

Subjects and Predicates .......................................... 70–72

Simple Subjects ........................................................... 73

Compound Subjects ............................................... 74, 75

Simple Predicates ....................................................... 76

Compound Predicates ........................................... 77, 78

Subjects ........................................................................ 79

Predicates .................................................................... 80

**Review** ...................................................................... **81**

Word Order ................................................................. 82

Sentences and Non-Sentences ............................... 83

Completing a Story ..................................................... 84

Complete the Sentences ...................................... 85, 86

Alliteration ................................................................... 87

Statements and Questions ..................................... 88, 89

Exclamations ............................................................... 90

**Review** ...................................................................... **91**

Contractions ............................................................... 92

Apostrophes ............................................................... 93

Quotation Marks ..................................................... 94, 95

**Review** ...................................................................... **96**

Acronyms ..................................................................... 97

Parts of a Paragraph ................................................. 98

Topic Sentences ......................................................... 99

Middle Sentences ..................................................... 100

Ending Sentences ..................................................... 101

**Review** .................................................................... **102**

Letter Writing ....................................................... 103, 104

Poetry .................................................................. 105, 106

Glossary ............................................................... 107–109

Answer Key .......................................................... 109–126

Teaching Suggestions ...................................... 127, 128

Name: _____

# Alphabetical Order

**Directions: Alphabetical order** is putting words in the order in which they appear in the alphabet. Put the eggs in alphabetical order. The first and last words are done for you.

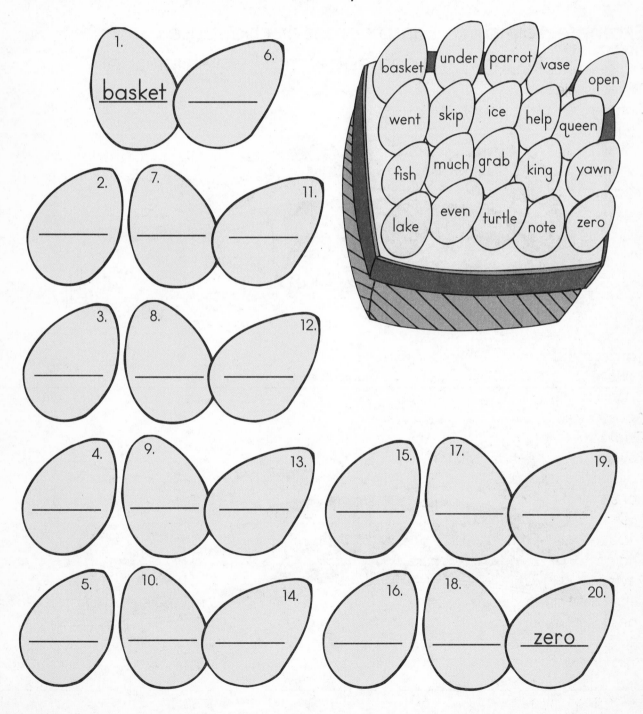

1. basket
6. _____

2. _____
7. _____
11. _____

3. _____
8. _____
12. _____

4. _____
9. _____
13. _____
15. _____
17. _____
19. _____

5. _____
10. _____
14. _____
16. _____
18. _____
20. zero

Basket words: basket, under, parrot, vase, open, went, skip, ice, help, queen, fish, much, grab, king, yawn, lake, even, turtle, note, zero

# Alphabetical Order

**Directions:** Write the words in alphabetical order. Look at the first letter of each word. If the first letter of two words is the same, look at the second letter.

**Example:** l(a)mp     Lamp comes first because

l(i)ght       **a** comes before **i** in the alphabet.

_____  _____  _____  _____  _____

_____  _____  _____  _____  _____

Name: _____

# Alphabetical Order

Arrange the words in alphabetical order by the first and second letters.

**Directions:** Read the words and circle the first letter of each word. Then write the words in alphabetical order on the bricks below.

apple
artist
zebra
xylophone
deer
night
pretty
elephant
catch
zipper
fund
touch
rain
lump
valentine
jelly
forest
horse

| | | |
|---|---|---|
| 1. | 2. | 3. |
| 4. | 5. | 6. |
| 7. | 8. | 9. |
| 10. | 11. | 12. |
| 13. | 14. | 15. |
| 16. | 17. | 18. |

Name: _____

# Compound Words

**Compound words** are two words that are put together to make one new word.

**Example:**

nut + shell = nutshell

**Directions:** Choose a word from the box to make compound words in the sentences below.

| board | bone | ground | prints | shake | house |
|-------|------|--------|--------|-------|-------|
| brush | man | top | shell | ball | hive |

**Example:**

The bird built its nest in the **treetop.**

1. We pitched our tent at the camp _____.

2. You would not be able to stand up without your back _____.

3. The police officer looked for finger _____.

4. She placed the hair _____in her purse.

5. It is important to have a firm hand _____.

6. The teacher wrote on the chalk _____.

7. The egg _____is cracked.

8. Our whole family plays foot _____together.

9. Be sure to put a top hat on the snow _____.

10. Spot never sleeps in his dog _____.

11. The beekeeper must check the bee _____ today.

Name: _____

# Compound Words

**Directions:** Write your own compound words by mixing up the words below. Add and subtract parts of each compound word to make up fun new compound words. Then draw pictures to illustrate your new words!

**Examples:**   **rattlesnake**   +   **starfish**   =   **rattlefish**
                 **junkyard**      +   **scarecrow**  =   **junkcrow**

| horseshoe | bedroom | moonlight | scarecrow |
| spaceship | seaweed | goldfish | mailbox |
| butterfly | farmhouse | sailboat | bodyguard |
| sunshine | sidewalk | lifeguard | junkyard |

_____     _____

_____     _____

_____     _____

_____     _____

_____     _____

# Antonyms

**Antonyms** are words that are opposites.

**Example:**  **hairy**  **bald**

**Directions:** Choose a word from the box to complete each sentence below.

| open | right | light | full | late | below |
|------|-------|-------|------|------|-------|
| hard | clean | slow | quiet | old | nice |

**Example:**

My car was dirty, but now it's **clean**.

1. Sometimes my cat is naughty, and sometimes she's _____.

2. The sign said, "Closed," but the door was _____.

3. Is the glass half empty or half_____?

4. I bought new shoes, but I like my _____ ones better.

5. Skating is easy for me, but_____ for my brother.

6. The sky is dark at night and_____during the day.

7. I like a noisy house, but my mother likes a _____one.

8. My friend says I'm wrong, but I say I'm _____.

9. Jason is a fast runner, but Adam is a _____runner.

10. We were supposed to be early, but we were_____.

Name: _____

# Antonyms

**Directions:** Write the antonym pairs from each sentence in the boxes.

**Example:** Many things are bought and sold at the market.

| bought | sold |
|---|---|

1. I thought I lost my dog, but someone found him.

| | |
|---|---|

2. The teacher will ask questions for the students to answer.

| | |
|---|---|

3. Airplanes arrive and depart from the airport.

| | |
|---|---|

4. The water in the pool was cold compared to the warm water in the whirlpool.

| | |
|---|---|

5. The tortoise was slow, but the hare was fast.

| | |
|---|---|

# Synonyms

**Synonyms** are words that mean almost the same thing.

**Example: small** and **little**

**Directions:** Look at the clues below. Complete the puzzle with words from the box that mean the same thing.

| pot | pretty | late | huge | close |
|-----|--------|------|------|-------|
| funny | smile | fast | unhappy | exit |

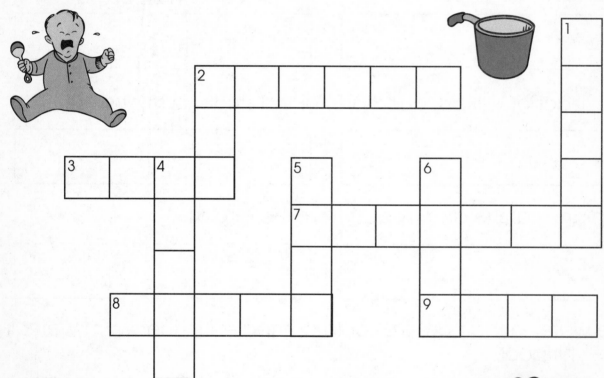

**Across:**

2. beautiful
3. quick
7. sad
8. near
9. leave

**Down:**

1. silly
2. pan
4. grin
5. big
6. tardy

Name: _____

# Synonyms

**Directions:** Match the pairs of synonyms.

delight •     • discover
speak •     • tidy
lovely •     • start
find •     • talk
nearly •     • beautiful
neat •     • almost
big •     • joy
sad •     • unhappy
begin •     • large

**Directions:** Read each sentence. Write the synonym pairs from each sentence in the boxes.

1. That unusual clock is a rare antique.

2. I am glad you are so happy!

3. Becky felt unhappy when she heard the sad news.

Name: _____

# Homophones

**Homophones** are words that sound the same but are spelled differently and have different meanings.

**Example:**

**sew**          **sow**          **so**

So what do I do now?

**Directions:** Read the sentences and write the correct word in the blanks.

**Example:**

**blue   blew**     She has **blue** eyes.

The wind **blew** the barn down.

**eye     I**     He hurt his left _____ playing ball.

_____ like to learn new things.

**see     sea**     Can you _____ the winning runner from here?

He goes diving for pearls under the _____ .

**eight   ate**     The baby _____ the banana.

Jane was _____ years old last year.

**one     won**     Jill _____ first prize at the science fair.

I am the only _____ in my family with red hair.

**be      bee**     Jenny cried when a _____ stung her.

I have to _____ in bed every night at eight o'clock.

**two  to  too**     My father likes _____ play tennis.

I like to play, _____ .

It takes at least _____ people to play.

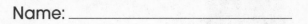

# Homophones

**Directions:** Read the clues below. Use the box to help you write the correct words in the puzzle.

## Across:

2. I was ___ from cheering at the football game.
3. You _____ the car to stop.
4. Another name for a **chicken**.
5. The boat had a _____.
6. I _____ my bed.
8. His _____ face told me he was sick.
9. My cat has a long _____.
10. The store had a _____.
11. To run away.
12. The _____ were at the zoo.

## Down:

1. Can you help me _____ the cheese?
2. An animal that "neighs."
3. _____ the egg to open it.
4. The _____ made my dog itch.
6. The _____ worked at the motel.
7. The _____ paper has comics.
8. The toddler used his shovel and _____ at the beach.
9. My favorite is the _____ of "Jack and the Beanstalk."
11. The baseball player hit a _____ ball.
12. Another word for **good**.

| | | | | | |
|---|---|---|---|---|---|
| pale | brake | flee | sale | gnus | flea | fowl |
| maid | pail | hoarse | foul | tail | sail | made |
| horse | tale | grate | break | great | news | |

Name: _____

# Review

**Directions:** Write the correct word to complete the sentences below.

**Their      There**      _____ suitcases were lost at the airport.

**ant      aunt**      My _____ and uncle are coming to visit.

**sale      sail**      My brother is learning to _____ .

**nose      knows**      Jenny _____ how to play a violin.

**pair      pear**      She put a ripe _____ in my lunchbox.

**Gentle      Early**      _____ means the same as **tame**.

**below      apart**      The opposite of **above** is _____ .

**Correct      Wet**      _____ means the same as **right**.

**Little      Dry**      _____ means the same as **small**.

**Wrong      Quick**      _____ means the same as **fast**.

**late      off**      The opposite of **on** is _____ .

**under      around**      The opposite of **over** is _____ .

Now, circle the first letter of each word you wrote above. Write the words in alphabetical order on the lines below.

1. _____      5. _____      9. _____

2. _____      6. _____      10. _____

3. _____      7. _____      11. _____

4. _____      8. _____      12. _____

Name: _____

# Nouns

**Nouns** are words that tell the names of people, places or things.

**Directions:** Read the words below. Then write them in the correct column.

| | | |
|---|---|---|
| goat | Mrs. Jackson | girl |
| beach | tree | song |
| mouth | park | Jean Rivers |
| finger | flower | New York |
| Kevin Jones | Elm City | Frank Gates |
| Main Street | theater | skates |
| River Park | father | boy |

**Person**

**Place**

**Thing**

_____    _____    _____

_____    _____    _____

_____    _____    _____

_____    _____    _____

_____    _____    _____

_____    _____    _____

_____    _____    _____

# Nouns

Nouns can also name ideas. **Ideas** are things we cannot see or touch such as bravery, beauty or honesty.

**Directions:** Underline the "idea" nouns in each sentence.

1. Respect is something that must be earned.

2. Truth and justice are two things that are highly valued.

3. The beauty of the flower garden was breathtaking.

4. Skills must be learned in order to master new things.

5. His courage impressed everyone.

Name: _____

# Common Nouns

**Common nouns** are nouns that name any member of a group of people, places or things, rather than specific people, places or things.

**Directions:** Read the sentences below and write the common noun found in each sentence.

**Example:** <u>socks</u> My socks do not match.

1. _____ The bird could not fly.

2. _____ Ben likes to eat jelly beans.

3. _____ I am going to meet my mother.

4. _____ We will go swimming in the lake tomorrow.

5. _____ I hope the flowers will grow quickly.

6. _____ We colored eggs together.

7. _____ It is easy to ride a bicycle.

8. _____ My cousin is very tall.

9. _____ Ted and Jane went fishing in their boat.

10. _____ They won a prize yesterday.

11. _____ She fell down and twisted her ankle.

12. _____ My brother was born today.

13. _____ She went down the slide.

14. _____ Ray went to the doctor today.

Name: _____

# Proper Nouns

**Proper nouns** are names of specific people, places or things. Proper nouns begin with a capital letter.

**Directions:** Read the sentences below and circle the proper nouns found in each sentence.

**Example:** (Aunt Frances) gave me a puppy for my birthday.

1. We lived on Jackson Street before we moved to our new house.

2. Angela's birthday party is tomorrow night.

3. We drove through Cheyenne, Wyoming on our way home.

4. Dr. Charles always gives me a treat for not crying.

5. George Washington was our first president.

6. Our class took a field trip to the Johnson Flower Farm.

7. Uncle Jack lives in New York City.

8. Amy and Elizabeth are best friends.

9. We buy doughnuts at the Grayson Bakery.

10. My favorite movie is *E.T.*

11. We flew to Miami, Florida in a plane.

12. We go to Riverfront Stadium to watch the baseball games.

13. Mr. Fields is a wonderful music teacher.

14. My best friend is Tom Dunlap.

# Proper Nouns

**Directions:** Rewrite each sentence, capitalizing the proper nouns.

1. mike's birthday is in september.

_____

2. aunt katie lives in detroit, michigan.

_____

3. In july, we went to canada.

_____

4. kathy jones moved to utah in january.

_____

5. My favorite holiday is valentine's day in february.

_____

6. On friday, mr. polzin gave the smith family a tour.

_____

7. saturday, uncle cliff and I will go to the mall of america in
   minnesota.

_____

_____

# Proper Nouns

**Directions:** Write about you! Write a proper noun for each category below. Capitalize the first letter of each proper noun.

1. Your first name: _____

2. Your last name: _____

3. Your street: _____

4. Your city: _____

5. Your state: _____

6. Your school: _____

7. Your best friend's name: _____

8. Your teacher: _____

9. Your favorite book character: _____

10. Your favorite vacation place: _____

Name: _____

# Common and Proper Nouns

**Directions:** Look at the list of nouns in the box. Write the common nouns under the kite. Write the proper nouns under the balloon. Remember to capitalize the first letter of each proper noun.

lisa smith

cats

shoelace

saturday

dr. martin

whistle

teddy bears

main street

may

boy

lawn chair

mary stewart

bird

florida

school

apples

washington, d.c.

pine cone

elizabeth jones

charley reynolds

Name: _____

# Plural Nouns

A **plural** is more than one person, place or thing. We usually add an **s** to show that a noun names more than one. If a noun ends in **x**, **ch**, **sh** or **s**, we add an **es** to the word.

Example:    *pizza*     *pizzas*

**Directions:** Write the plural of the words below.

**Example: dog + s = dogs**

cat  _____

boot  _____

house  _____

**Example: ax + es = axes**

fox  _____

tax  _____

box  _____

**Example: dish + es = dishes**

bush  _____

ash  _____

brush  _____

**Example: peach + es = peaches**

lunch  _____

bunch  _____

punch  _____

**Example: glass + es = glasses**

mess  _____

guess  _____

class  _____

**walrus**

**walruses**

# Plural Nouns

To write the plural forms of words ending in **y**, we change the **y** to **ie** and add **s**.

**Example:** pony ___*ponies*___

**Directions:** Write the plural of each noun on the lines below.

berry     _____

cherry    _____

bunny    _____

penny     _____

family     _____

candy     _____

party      _____

Now, write a story using some of the words that end in **y**. Remember to use capital letters and periods.

_____

_____

_____

_____

Name: _____

# Plural Nouns

**Directions:** Write the plural of each noun to complete the sentences below. Remember to change the **y** to **ie** before you add **s**!

1. I am going to two birthday _____ this week.
   (party)

2. Sandy picked some _____ for Mom's pie.
   (cherry)

3. At the store, we saw lots of _____.
   (bunny)

4. My change at the candy store was three _____.
   (penny)

5. All the _____ baked cookies for the bake sale.
   (lady)

6. Thanksgiving is a special time for _____ to gather together.
   (family)

7. Boston and New York are very large _____.
   (city)

# Plural Nouns

Some words have special plural forms.

**Example:**   leaf        leaves

**Directions:** Some of the words in the box are special plurals. Complete each sentence with a plural from the box. Then write the letters from the boxes in the blanks below to solve the puzzle.

| | |
|---|---|
| tooth | teeth |
| child | children |
| foot | feet |
| mouse | mice |
| woman | women |
| man | men |

1. I lost my two front ___ ___ ___ [ ] ___ !

2. My sister has two pet ___ ___ [ ] .

3. Her favorite book is Little ___ ___ [ ] .

4. The circus clown had big ___ ___ [ ] .

5. The teacher played a game with the [ ] ___ ___ ___ ___ ___ .

Take good care of this pearly plural!

___ ___ ___ ___ ___
 1   2   3   4   5

# Plural Nouns

**Directions:** The **singular form** of a word shows one person, place or thing. Write the singular form of each noun on the lines below.

cherries _____

lunches _____

countries _____

leaves _____

churches _____

arms _____

boxes _____

men _____

wheels _____

pictures _____

cities _____

places _____

ostriches _____

glasses _____

Name: _____

# Review

**Directions:** Circle the common nouns in each sentence. Underline the proper nouns. Then write the plural form of each common noun on the lines below.

**What would you take on a space ship?**

1. Jason will take his bicycle and his radio.

2. Lauren says she cannot live without her pet.

3. Max will take his lunch.

4. Charlie and Greg are taking a game and a television.

5. Katie wants to take the entire city of Nashville, Tennessee.

6. Jack's mother said he could take his messy room with him.

7. Andy wants his teacher, Mr. Temple to go with him.

8. Jessica wants to take a neighbor from Mulberry Street.

9. Jill likes to swim and is taking the Metro City Pool with her.

10. I think I am going to take my dog, Mr. Buster, with me.

_____

_____

_____

_____     _____     _____

_____     _____     _____

_____     _____     _____

Name: _____

# Possessive Nouns

**Possessive nouns** tell who or what is the owner of something. With singular nouns, we use an apostrophe **before** the **s**. With plural nouns, we use an apostrophe **after** the **s**.

**Example:**

singular: one elephant

The **elephant's** dance was wonderful.

plural: more than one elephant

The **elephants'** dance was wonderful.

**Directions:** Put the apostrophe in the correct place in each bold word. Then write the word in the blank.

1. The **lions** cage was big. _____

2. The **bears** costumes were purple. _____

3. One **boys** laughter was very loud. _____

4. The **trainers** dogs were dancing about. _____

5. The **mans** popcorn was tasty and good. _____

6. **Marks** cotton candy was delicious. _____

7. A little **girls** balloon burst in the air. _____

8. The big **clowns** tricks were very funny. _____

9. **Lauras** sister clapped for the clowns. _____

10. The **womans** money was lost in the crowd. _____

11. **Kellys** mother picked her up early. _____

Name: _____

# Possessive Nouns

**Directions:** Circle the correct possessive noun in each sentence and write it in the blank.

**Example:** One ___*girl's*___ mother is a teacher.

　　　　(girl's)　　girls'

1. The _____ tail is long.

　　cat's　　　　cats'

2. One _____ baseball bat is aluminum.

　　boy's　　　　boys'

3. A _____ aprons are white.

　　waitresses'　　waitress's

4. My _____ apple pie is the best!

　　grandmother's　　grandmothers'

5. My five _____ uniforms are dirty.

　　brother's　　brothers'

6. The _____ doll is pretty.

　　child's　　　childs'

7. This _____ collars are different colors.

　　dog's　　　dogs'

8. The _____ tail is short.

　　cow's　　　cows'

# Pronouns

**Pronouns** are words that are used in place of nouns.
**Examples:** **he, she, it, they, him, them, her, him**

**Directions:** Read each sentence. Write the pronoun that takes the place of each noun.

**Example:**
  The **monkey** dropped the banana. _It_

1. **Dad** washed the car last night. _____

2. **Mary and David** took a walk in the park. _____

3. **Peggy** spent the night at her grandmother's house. _____

4. The baseball **players** lost their game. _____

5. **Mike Van Meter** is a great soccer player. _____

6. The **parrot** can say five different words. _____

7. **Megan** wrote a story in class today. _____

8. They gave a party for **Teresa**. _____

9. Everyone in the class was happy for **Ted**. _____

10. The children petted the **giraffe**. _____

11. Linda put the **kittens** near the warm stove. _____

12. **Gina** made a chocolate cake for my birthday. _____

13. **Pete and Matt** played baseball on the same team. _____

14. Give the books to **Herbie**. _____

Name: _____

# Pronouns

**Singular Pronouns**

I  me  my  mine

you  your  yours

he  she  it  her

hers  his  its  him

**Plural Pronouns**

we  us  our  ours

you  your  yours

they  them  their  theirs

**Directions:** Underline the pronouns in each sentence.

1. Mom told us to wash our hands.

2. Did you go to the store?

3. We should buy him a present.

4. I called you about their party.

5. Our house had damage on its roof.

6. They want to give you a prize at our party.

7. My cat ate her sandwich.

8. Your coat looks like his coat.

Name: _____

# Pronouns

We use the pronouns **I** and **we** when talking about the person or people doing the action.

**Example:** **I** can roller skate. **We** can roller skate.

We use **me** and **us** when talking about something that is happening to a person or people.

**Example:** They gave **me** the roller skates.
They gave **us** the roller skates.

**Directions:** Circle the correct pronoun and write it in the blank.

**Example:**

_We_ are going to the picnic together.                    (We,) Us

1. _____ am finished with my science project.          I, Me

2. Eric passed the football to _____ .                 me, I

3. They ate dinner with _____ last night.              we, us

4. _____ like spinach better than ice cream.           I, Me

5. Mom came in the room to tell _____ good night.      me, I

6. _____ had a pizza party in our backyard.            Us, We

7. They told _____ the good news.                      us, we

8. Tom and _____ went to the store.                    me, I

9. She is taking _____ with her to the movies.         I, me

10. Katie and _____ are good friends.                  I, me

Name: _____

# Possessive Pronouns

**Possessive pronouns** show ownership.

**Example: his** hat, **her** shoes, **our** dog

We can use these pronouns before a noun:
**my, our, you, his, her, its, their**

**Example:** That is **my** bike.

We can use these pronouns on their own:
**mine, yours, ours, his, hers, theirs, its**

**Example:** That is **mine**.

**Directions:** Write each sentence again, using a pronoun instead of the words in bold letters. Be sure to use capitals and periods.

**Example:**

My **dog's** bowl is brown.        **Its** bowl is brown.

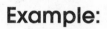

1. That is **Lisa's** book. _____

2. This is **my pencil.** _____

3. This hat is **your hat**. _____

4. Fifi is **Kevin's** cat. _____

5. That beautiful house is **our home**.

_____

6. **The gerbil's** cage is too small.

_____

Name: _____

# Abbreviations

An **abbreviation** is the shortened form of a word. Most abbreviations begin with a capital letter and end with a period.

| | | | |
|---|---|---|---|
| Mr. | Mister | St. | Street |
| Mrs. | Missus | Ave. | Avenue |
| Dr. | Doctor | Blvd. | Boulevard |
| A.M. | before noon | Rd. | Road |
| P.M. | after noon | | |

Days of the week: Sun. Mon. Tues. Wed. Thurs. Fri. Sat.
Months of the year: Jan. Feb. Mar. Apr. Aug. Sept. Oct. Nov. Dec.

**Directions:** Write the abbreviations for each word.

street _____   doctor _____   Tuesday _____

road _____   mister _____   avenue _____

missus _____   October _____   Friday _____

before noon _____   March _____   August _____

**Directions:** Write each sentence using abbreviations.

1. On Monday at 9:00 before noon Mister Jones had a meeting.

_____

2. In December Doctor Carlson saw Missus Zuckerman.

_____

3. One Tuesday in August Mister Wood went to the park.

_____

Name: _____

# Adjectives

**Adjectives** are words that tell more about nouns, such as a **happy** child, a **cold** day or a **hard** problem. Adjectives can tell how many (**one** airplane) or which one (**those** shoes).

**Directions:** The nouns are in bold letters. Circle the adjectives that describe the nouns.

**Example:** Some people have (unusual) **pets**.

1. Some people keep wild **animals**, like lions and bears.

2. These **pets** need special care.

3. These **animals** want to be free when they get older.

4. Even small **animals** can be difficult if they are wild.

5. Raccoons and squirrels are not tame **pets**.

6. Never touch a wild **animal** that may be sick.

Complete the story below by writing in your own adjectives. Use your imagination.

## My Cat

My cat is a very_____ animal. She has _____

and _____ fur. Her favorite toy is a _____ ball.

She has _____ claws. She has a _____ tail.

She has a _____ face and _____ whiskers.

I think she is the _____ cat in the world!

Name: _____

# Adjectives

**Directions:** Read the story below and underline the adjectives which are used in the story.

### The Best Soup I Ever Had

I woke up one cold winter morning and decided to make a delicious pot of hot vegetable soup. The first vegetables I put in the big grey pot were some sweet white onions. Then I added orange carrots and dark green broccoli. The broccoli looked just like little, tiny trees. Fresh, juicy tomatoes and crisp potatoes were added next. I cooked it for a long, long time. This soup turned out to be the best soup I ever had.

Write two adjectives to describe each of the words below.

cucumber _____long_____        peas _____

_____green_____        _____

spinach _____        corn _____

_____        _____

Now, rewrite two of the sentences from the story. Substitute your own adjectives for the words you underlined to make your own soup.

_____

_____

_____

Name: _____

# Adjectives and Nouns

**Directions:** Underline the noun in each sentence below. Then draw an arrow from each adjective to the noun it describes.

**Example:**

A platypus is a furry <u>animal</u> that lives in Australia.

1. This animal likes to swim.

2. The nose looks like a duck's bill.

3. It has a broad tail like a beaver.

4. Platypuses are great swimmers.

5. They have webbed feet which help them swim.

6. Their flat tails also help them move through the water.

7. The platypus is an unusual mammal because it lays eggs.

8. The eggs look like reptile eggs.

9. Platypuses can lay three eggs at a time.

10. These babies do not leave their mothers for one year.

11. This animal spends most of its time hunting near streams.

# Adjectives

A chart of adjectives can also be used to help describe nouns.

**Directions:** Look at the pictures. Complete each chart.

**Example:**

| Noun | What Color? | What Size? | What Number? |
|---|---|---|---|
| flower | red | small | two |

| Noun | What Color? | What Size? | What Number? |
|---|---|---|---|
|  |  |  |  |

| Noun | What Color? | What Size? | What Number? |
|---|---|---|---|
|  |  |  |  |

| Noun | What Color? | What Size? | What Number? |
|---|---|---|---|
|  |  |  |  |

# Prefixes

**Prefixes** are special word parts added to the beginnings of words. Prefixes change the meaning of words.

| Prefix | Meaning | Example |
|--------|---------|---------|
| un | not | **un**happy |
| re | again | **re**do |
| pre | before | **pre**view |
| mis | wrong | **mis**understanding |
| dis | opposite | **dis**obey |

**Directions:** Circle the word that begins with a prefix. Then write the prefix and the root word.

1. The dog was unfriendly.  _____ + _____

2. The movie preview was interesting.  _____ + _____

3. The referee called an unfair penalty.  _____ + _____

4. Please do not misbehave.  _____ + _____

5. My parents disapprove of that show.  _____ + _____

6. I had to redo the assignment.  _____ + _____

Name: _____

# Suffixes

**Suffixes** are word parts added to the ends of words. Suffixes change the meaning of words.

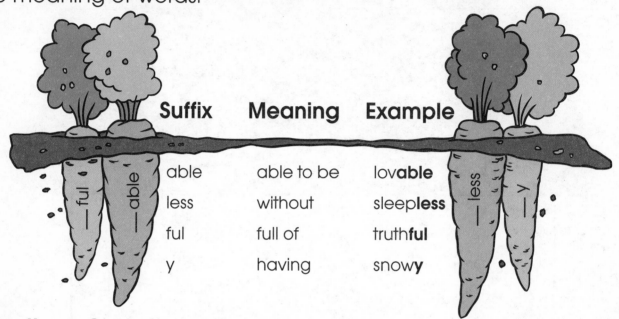

| Suffix | Meaning | Example |
|--------|---------|---------|
| able | able to be | lov**able** |
| less | without | sleep**less** |
| ful | full of | truth**ful** |
| y | having | snow**y** |

**Directions:** Circle the suffix in each word below.

**Example:** fluff(y)

| | | |
|---|---|---|
| rainy | thoughtful | likeable |
| blameless | enjoyable | helpful |
| peaceful | careless | silky |

**Directions:** Write a word for each meaning.

full of hope _____    having rain _____

without hope _____    able to break _____

without power _____    full of cheer _____

Name: _____

# Review

**Directions:** Circle the nouns that show ownership. Draw a box around the pronouns. Underline the adjectives. An example of each is done for you.

**Example:**

<u>Tropical</u> birds live in <u>warm</u>, <u>wet</u> lands.

1. [They] live in dark forests and busy zoos.

2. Their feathers are bright.

3. A canary is a small finch.

4. It is named for the Canary Islands.

5. (Ben's) birds are lovebirds.

6. He says they are small parrots that like to cuddle.

7. His parents gave him the lovebirds for his birthday.

8. Lisa's bird is a talking myna bird.

9. Her neighbors gave it to her when they moved.

10. She thanked them for the wonderful gift.

11. She says its feathers are dark with an orange mark on each wing.

12. Some children's myna birds can be very noisy.

13. Parakeets are this country's most popular tropical birds.

14. Parakeets' cages have ladders and swings.

15. A parakeet's diet is made up of seeds.

Name: _____

# Verbs

A **verb** is the action word in a sentence, the word that tells what something does or that something exists. **Examples: run, jump, skip.**

**Directions:** Draw a box around the verb in each sentence below.

1. Spiders spin webs of silk.

2. A spider waits in the center of the web for its meals.

3. A spider sinks its sharp fangs into insects.

4. Spiders eat many insects.

5. Spiders make their nests with silk.

6. Female spiders wrap silk around their eggs to protect them.

**Directions:** Choose the correct verb from the box and write it in the sentences below.

| hides | swims | eats | grabs | hurt |
|-------|-------|------|-------|------|

1. A crab spider _____ deep inside a flower where it cannot be seen.

2. The crab spider _____ insects when they land on the flower.

3. The wolf spider is good because it _____ wasps.

4. The water spider _____ under water.

5. Most spiders will not _____ people.

Name: _____

# Verbs

When a verb tells what one person or thing is doing now, it usually ends in **s**. **Example:** She **sings**.

When a verb is used with **you**, **I** or **we**, we do not add an **s**.

**Example:** I **sing**.

**Directions:** Write the correct verb in each sentence.

**Example:**

I ___write___ a newspaper about our street.        **writes, write**

1. My sister _____ me sometimes.        **helps, help**

2. She _____ the pictures.        **draw, draws**

3. We _____ them together.        **delivers, deliver**

4. I _____ the news about all the people.        **tell, tells**

5. Mr. Macon _____ the most beautiful flowers.        **grow, grows**

6. Mrs. Jones _____ to her plants.        **talks, talk**

7. Kevin Turner _____ his dog loose everyday.        **lets, let**

8. Little Mikey Smith _____ lost once a week.        **get, gets**

9. You may _____ I live on an interesting street.        **thinks, think**

10. We _____ it's the best street in town.        **say, says**

# Helping Verbs

A **helping verb** is a word used with an action verb.

**Examples: might**, **shall** and **are**

**Directions:** Write a helping verb from the box with each action verb.

| can | could | must | might |
|-----|-------|------|-------|
| may | would | should | will |
| shall | did | does | do |
| had | have | has | am |
| are | were | is | |
| be | being | been | |

**Example:**

Tomorrow, I _____ **might** _____ play soccer.

1. Mom _____ buy my new soccer shoes tonight.

2. Yesterday, my old soccer shoes _____ ripped by the cat.

3. I _____ going to ask my brother to go to the game.

4. He usually _____ not like soccer.

5. But, he _____ go with me because I am his sister.

6. He _____ promised to watch the entire soccer game.

7. He has _____ helping me with my homework.

8. I _____ spell a lot better because of his help.

9. Maybe I _____ finish the semester at the top of my class.

# Past-Tense Verbs

The **past tense** of a verb tells about something that has already happened. We add a **d** or an **ed** to most verbs to show that something has already happened.

**Directions:** Use the verb from the first sentence to complete the second sentence.

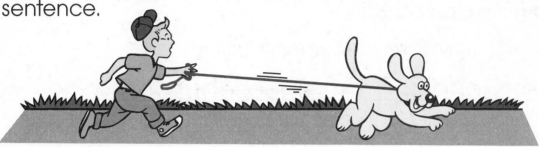

**Example:**

    Please **walk** the dog.    I already __walked__ her.

1. The flowers look good.    They _____ better yesterday.

2. Please accept my gift.    I _____ it for my sister.

3. I wonder who will win.    I _____ about it all night.

4. He will saw the wood.    He _____ some last week.

5. Fold the paper neatly.    She _____ her paper.

6. Let's cook outside tonight.    We _____ outside last night.

7. Do not block the way.    They _____ the entire street.

8. Form the clay this way.    He _____ it into a ball.

9. Follow my car.    We _____ them down the street.

10. Glue the pages like this.    She _____ the flowers on.

# Present-Tense Verbs

The **present tense** of a verb tells about something that is happening now, happens often or is about to happen. These verbs can be written two ways: The bird sing**s**. The bird is sing**ing**.

**Directions:** Write each sentence again, using the verb **is** and writing the **ing** form of the verb.

**Example:** He cooks the cheeseburgers.

<u>He is cooking the cheeseburgers.</u>

1. Sharon dances to that song.

_____

2. Frank washed the car.

_____

3. Mr. Benson smiles at me.

_____

Write a verb for the sentences below that tells something that is happening now. Be sure to use the verb **is** and the **ing** form of the verb.

**Example:** The big, brown dog <u>is barking</u>.

1. The little baby _____.

2. Most nine-year-olds _____.

3. The monster on television _____.

# Future-Tense Verbs

The **future tense** of a verb tells about something that has not happened yet but will happen in the future. **Will** or **shall** are usually used with future tense.

**Directions:** Change the verb tense in each sentence to future tense.

**Example:** She cooks dinner.

_She will cook dinner._

1. He plays baseball.

_____

2. She walks to school.

_____

3. Bobby talks to the teacher.

_____

4. I remember to vote.

_____

5. Jack mows the lawn every week.

_____

6. We go on vacation soon.

_____

# Review

**Verb tenses** can be in the past, present or future.

**Directions:** Match each sentence with the correct verb tense. (**Think:** When did each thing happen?)

It will rain tomorrow.              past                **Past**

He played golf.                     present

Molly is sleeping.                  future              **Present**

Jack is singing a song.             past

I shall buy a kite.                 present             **Future**

Dad worked hard today.              future

**Directions:** Change the verb to the tense shown.

1. Jenny played with her new friend. (present)

_____

2. Bobby is talking to him. (future)

_____

3. Holly and Angie walk here. (past)

_____

Name: _____

# Irregular Verbs

**Irregular verbs** are verbs that do not change from the present tense to the past tense in the regular way with **d** or **ed**.

**Example:** sing, **sang**

**Directions:** Read the sentence and underline the verbs. Choose the past-tense form from the box and write it next to the sentence.

| | |
|---|---|
| blow — blew | fly — flew |
| come — came | give — gave |
| take — took | wear — wore |
| make — made | sing — sang |
| grow — grew | |

**Example:**

Dad will <u>make</u> a cake tonight.                     _made_

1. I will probably grow another inch this year.     _____

2. I will blow out the candles.                     _____

3. Everyone will give me presents.                     _____

4. I will wear my favorite red shirt.                     _____

5. My cousins will come from out of town.                     _____

6. It will take them four hours.                     _____

7. My Aunt Betty will fly in from Cleveland.                     _____

8. She will sing me a song when she gets here.     _____

Name: _____

# Irregular Verbs

**Directions:** Circle the verb that completes each sentence.

1. Scientists will try to (find, found) the cure.

2. Eric (brings, brought) his lunch to school yesterday.

3. Everyday, Betsy (sings, sang) all the way home.

4. Jason (breaks, broke) the vase last night.

5. The ice had (freezes, frozen) in the tray.

6. Mitzi has (swims, swum) in that pool before.

7. Now I (choose, chose) to exercise daily.

8. The teacher has (rings, rung) the bell.

9. The boss (speaks, spoke) to us yesterday.

10. She (says, said) it twice already.

# Irregular Verbs

The verb **be** is different from all other verbs. The present-tense forms of **be** are **am**, **is** and **are**. The past-tense forms of **be** are **was** and **were**. The verb **to be** is written in the following ways:

**singular:** I am, you are, he is, she is, it is
**plural:** we are, you are, they are

**Directions:** Choose the correct form of **be** from the words in the box and write it in each sentence.

| are | am | is | was | were |
|-----|-----|-----|-----|-----|

**Example:**

I _____ **am** _____ feeling good at this moment.

1. My sister _____ a good singer.

2. You _____ going to the store with me.

3. Sandy _____ at the movies last week.

4. Rick and Tom _____ best friends.

5. He _____ happy about the surprise.

6. The cat _____ hungry.

7. I _____ going to the ball game.

8. They _____ silly.

9. I _____ glad to help my mother.

Name: _____

# Linking Verbs

**Linking verbs** connect the noun to a descriptive word. Linking verbs are often forms of the verb **be**.

**Directions:** The linking verb is underlined in each sentence. Circle the two words that are being connected.

**Example:** The (cat) <u>is</u> (fat.)

1. My favorite food <u>is</u> pizza.

2. The car <u>was</u> red.

3. I <u>am</u> tired.

4. Books <u>are</u> fun!

5. The garden <u>is</u> beautiful.

6. Pears <u>taste</u> juicy.

7. The airplane <u>looks</u> large.

8. Rabbits <u>are</u> furry.

Name: _____

# Review

**Directions:** Write the correct verb in each sentence below.

1. Before the wheel, people _____ heavy loads.  **drag, dragged**

2. No one knows who _____ the wheel.  **invented, invent**

3. The Sumerians _____ some of the first people to use the wheel.  **were, are**

4. They _____ the first wheels of wood and stone.  **make, made**

5. The wheels _____ very heavy.  **be, were**

6. Then people _____ of spokes.  **think, thought**

7. Spokes helped the wheels _____ more easily.  **turn, turned**

8. Soon, people were _____ roads.  **built, building**

9. I _____ glad that the wheel was invented.  **is, am**

10. We _____ many things with wheels.  **has, have**

11. Cars and trucks _____ wheels.  **has, have**

12. Potters _____ pots on a wheel.  **make, made**

13. Wool is _____ on a spinning wheel.  **spin, spun**

14. Amusement park rides _____ wheels.  **have, has**

15. My favorite set of wheels _____ on my bike.  **is, am**

Name: _____

# Adverbs

**Adverbs** are words that describe verbs. They tell where, how or when.

**Directions:** Circle the adverb in each of the following sentences.

**Example:** The doctor worked (carefully.)

1. The skater moved gracefully across the ice.

2. Their call was returned quickly.

3. We easily learned the new words.

4. He did the work perfectly.

5. She lost her purse somewhere.

Complete the sentences below by writing your own adverbs in the blanks.

**Example:** The bees worked _____busily_____.

1. The dog barked _____.

2. The baby smiled _____.

3. She wrote her name _____.

4. The horse ran _____.

# Adverbs

**Directions:** Read each sentence. Then answer the questions on the lines below.

**Example:** Charles ate hungrily.

who? _____Charles_____

what? _____ate_____     how? _____hungrily_____

1. She dances slowly.

who? _____

what? _____     how? _____

2. The girl spoke carefully.

who? _____

what? _____     how? _____

3. My brother ran quickly.

who? _____

what? _____     how? _____

4. Jean walks home often.

who? _____

what? _____     when? _____

5. The children played there.

who? _____

what? _____     where? _____

Name: _____

# Prepositions

**Prepositions** show relationships between the noun or pronoun and another noun in the sentence. The preposition comes before that noun.

**Example:** The <u>book</u> is (on) the table.

### Common Prepositions

| | | | | |
|---|---|---|---|---|
| above | behind | by | near | over |
| across | below | in | off | through |
| around | beside | inside | on | under |

**Directions:** Circle the prepositions in each sentence.

1. The dog ran fast around the house.

2. The plates in the cupboard were clean.

3. Put the card inside the envelope.

4. The towel on the sink was wet.

5. I planted flowers in my garden.

6. My kite flew high above the trees.

7. The chair near the counter was sticky.

8. Under the ground, worms lived in their homes.

9. I put the bow around the box.

10. Beside the pond, there was a playground.

Name: _____

# Articles

**Articles** are words used before nouns. **A**, **an** and **the** are articles. We use **a** before words that begin with a consonant. We use **an** before words that begin with a vowel.

**Example:**        **a peach**           **an apple**

**Directions:** Write **a** or **an** in the sentences below.

**Example:** My bike had _____**a**_____ flat tire.

1. They brought _____ goat to the farm.

2. My mom wears _____ old pair of shoes to mow the lawn.

3. We had _____ party for my grandfather.

4. Everybody had _____ ice-cream cone after the game.

5. We bought _____ picnic table for our backyard.

6. We saw _____ lion sleeping in the shade.

7. It was _____ evening to be remembered.

8. He brought _____ blanket to the game.

9. _____ exit sign was above the door.

10. They went to _____ orchard to pick apples.

11. He ate _____ orange for lunch.

Name: _____

# Commas

**Commas** are used to separate words in a series of three or more.

**Example:** My favorite fruits are apples, bananas and oranges.

**Directions:** Put commas where they are needed in each sentence.

1. Please buy milk eggs bread and cheese.

2. I need a folder paper and pencils for school.

3. Some good pets are cats dogs gerbils fish and rabbits.

4. Aaron Mike and Matt went to the baseball game.

5. Major forms of transportation are planes trains and automobiles.

Name: _____

# Articles and Commas

**Directions:** Write **a** or **an** in each blank. Put commas where they are needed in the paragraphs below.

### Owls

_____ owl is _____ bird of prey. This means it hunts

small animals. Owls catch insects fish and birds. Mice are

_____ owl's favorite dinner. Owls like protected places,

such as trees burrows or barns. Owls make noises that sound

like hoots screeches or even barks. _____ owl's feathers

may be black brown gray or white.

  **A Zoo for You**

_____ zoo is _____ excellent place for keeping animals. Zoos have

mammals birds reptiles and amphibians. Some zoos have domestic animals,

such as rabbits sheep and goats. Another name for this type of zoo is _____

petting zoo. In some zoos, elephants lions and tigers live in open country.

This is because _____ enormous animal needs open space for roaming.

Name: _____

# Commas

We use commas to separate the day from the year.
**Example:** May 13, 1950

**Directions:** Write the dates in the blanks. Put the
commas in and capitalize the name of each month.

**Example:**

Jack and Dave were born on february 22 1982.

_____February 22, 1982_____

1. My father's birthday is may 19 1948.

_____

2. My sister was fourteen on december 13 1994.

_____

3. Lauren's seventh birthday was on november 30 1998.

_____

4. october 13 1996 was the last day I saw my lost cat.

_____

5. On april 17 1997, we saw the Grand Canyon.

_____

6. Our vacation lasted from april 2 1998 to april 26 1998.

_____     _____

7. Molly's baby sister was born on august 14 1991.

_____

8. My mother was born on june 22 1959.

_____

Name: _____

# Capitalization

The names of **people**, **places** and **pets**, the **days of the week**, the **months of the year** and **holidays** begin with a capital letter.

**Directions:** Read the words in the box. Write the words in the correct column with capital letters at the beginning of each word.

| | | | |
|---|---|---|---|
| ron polsky | tuesday | march | april |
| presidents' day | saturday | woofy | october |
| blackie | portland, oregon | corning, new york | molly yoder |
| valentine's day | fluffy | harold edwards | arbor day |
| bozeman, montana | sunday | | |

**People**

_____

_____

_____

**Places**

_____

_____

_____

**Pets**

_____

_____

_____

**Days**

_____

_____

_____

**Months**

_____

_____

_____

**Holidays**

_____

_____

_____

Name: _____

# Commas

We capitalize the names of cities and states. We use a comma to separate the name of a city and a state.

**Directions:** Use capital letters and commas to write the names of the cities and states correctly.

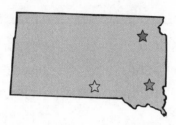

**Example:**

sioux falls south dakota ____Sioux Falls, South Dakota____

1. plymouth massachusetts _____

2. boston massachusetts _____

3. philadelphia pennsylvania _____

4. white plains new york _____

5. newport rhode island _____

6. yorktown virginia _____

7. nashville tennessee _____

8. portland oregon _____

9. mansfield ohio _____

Name: _____

# Review

**Directions:** Write an adverb from the box in the sentences below to tell how, when or where something happens.

| merrily | carefully | thoroughly | there | always | sometimes |
|---|---|---|---|---|---|

1. The coach always makes us stretch our muscles _____ (**how?**).

2. Katie is _____ (**when?**) the perfect guest when she visits.

3. The canaries sang _____ (**how?**) in their cages.

4. He hit the ball way over _____ (**where?**).

**Directions:** Read the words in the box. Circle the word if **an** should be used as the article before the word. Underline the word if **a** should be used as the article before the word.

| bath | cake | owl | apple | ice | cookie |
|---|---|---|---|---|---|
| beach | umbrella | onion | oven | dress | shoe |
| girl | boy | egg | elf | foot | book |

**Directions:** Use commas and capital letters to write the following dates and places correctly.

1. february 6 1996 _____

2. johnson wisconsin _____

3. september 20 1998 _____

4. cheyenne wyoming _____

Name: _____

# Parts of Speech

Nouns, pronouns, verbs, adjectives, adverbs and prepositions are all **parts of speech**.

**Directions:** Label the words in each sentence with the correct part of speech.

**Example:**

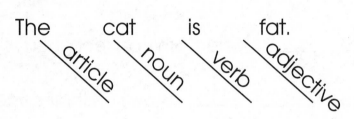

The     cat     is     fat.
 article  noun   verb  adjective

1. My     cow     walks     in     the     barn.

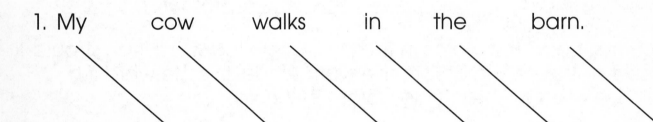

2. Red     flowers     grow     in     the     garden.

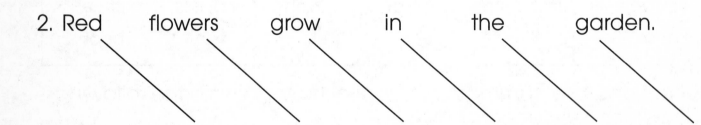

3. The     large     dog     was     excited.

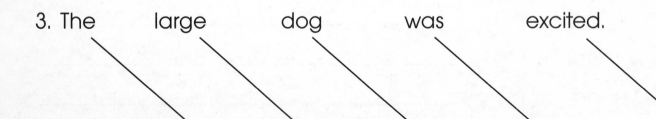

Name: _____

# Parts of Speech

**Directions:** Ask someone to give you nouns, verbs, adjectives and pronouns where shown. Write them in the blanks. Read the story to your friend when you finish.

**The** _____ **Adventure**
          (adjective)

I went for a _____ . I found a really big _____ .
              (noun)                                    (noun)

It was so _____ that I _____ all the
            (adjective)                    (verb)

way home. I put it in my _____ . To my amazement, it
                           (noun)

began to _____ . I _____ . I took it to my
           (verb)          (past-tense verb)

_____ . I showed it to all my _____ .
  (place)                                (plural noun)

I decided to _____ it in a box and wrap it up with
               (verb)

_____ paper. I gave it to _____ for a
  (adjective)                        (person)

present. When _____ opened it, _____
                (pronoun)                     (pronoun)

_____ . _____ shouted, "Thank you!
  (past-tense verb)    (pronoun)

This is the best _____ I've ever had!"
                   (noun)

Name: _____

# Parts of Speech

**Directions:** Write the part of speech of each underlined word.

NOUN PRONOUN VERB ADJECTIVE ADVERB PREPOSITION

①　　②
There <u>are</u> many <u>different</u> kinds of animals. Some animals live in the

③
wild. Some animals live in the <u>zoo</u>. And still others live in homes. The animals

④
that <u>live</u> in homes are called pets.

There are many types of pets. Some pets without fur are fish, turtles,

⑤　　⑥
snakes and hermit crabs. Trained birds can fly <u>around</u> <u>your</u> house. Some

⑦
<u>furry</u> animals are cats, dogs, rabbits, ferrets, gerbils or hamsters. Some animals

⑧　　　　　⑨
can <u>successfully</u> learn tricks that <u>you</u> teach them. Whatever your favorite

⑩
animal is, animals can be <u>special</u> friends!

1. _____　4. _____

2. _____　5. _____　7. _____　9. _____

3. _____　6. _____　8. _____　10. _____

Name: _____

# And and But

We can use **and** or **but** to make one longer sentence from two short ones.

**Directions:** Use **and** or **but** to make two short sentences into a longer, more interesting one. Write the new sentence on the line below the two short sentences.

**Example:**

The skunk has black fur. The skunk has a white stripe.

_The skunk has black fur and a white stripe._

1. The skunk has a small head. The skunk has small ears.

_____

2. The skunk has short legs. Skunks can move quickly.

_____

3. Skunks sleep in hollow trees. Skunk sleep underground.

_____

4. Skunks are chased by animals. Skunks do not run away.

_____

5. Skunks sleep during the day. Skunks hunt at night.

_____

# Subjects

A **subject** tells who or what the sentence is about.

**Directions:** Underline the subject in the following sentences.

**Example:**

<u>The zebra</u> is a large animal.

1. Zebras live in Africa.

2. Zebras are related to horses.

3. Horses have longer hair than zebras.

4. Zebras are good runners.

5. Their feet are protected by their hooves.

6. Some animals live in groups.

7. These groups are called herds.

8. Zebras live in herds with other grazing animals.

9. Grazing animals eat mostly grass.

10. They usually eat three times a day.

11. They often travel to water holes.

Name: _____

# Predicates

A **predicate** tells what the subject is doing, has done or will do.

**Directions:** Underline the predicate in the following sentences.

**Example:** Woodpeckers <u>live in trees.</u>

1. They hunt for insects in the trees.

2. Woodpeckers have strong beaks.

3. They can peck through the bark.

4. The pecking sound can be heard from far away.

**Directions:** Circle the groups of words that can be predicates.

have long tongues              pick up insects

hole in bark                   sticky substance

help it to climb trees         tree bark

Now, choose the correct predicates from above to finish these sentences.

1. Woodpeckers _____ .

2. They use their tongues to _____ .

3. Its strong feet _____ .

Name: ____________________

# Subjects and Predicates

**Directions:** Write the words for the subject to answer the **who** or **what** questions. Write the words for the predicate to answer the **does, did, is** or **has** questions.

**Example:**

My friend has two pairs of sunglasses. **who?** My friend

**has?** has two pairs of sunglasses.

1. John's dog went to school with him. **what?** ____________

   **did?** ____________

2. The Eskimo traveled by dog sled. **who?** ____________

   **did?** ____________

3. Alex slept in his treehouse last night. **who?** ____________

   **did?** ____________

4. Cherry pie is my favorite kind of pie. **what?** ____________

   **is?** ____________

5. The mail carrier brings the mail to the door. **who?** ____________

   **does?** ____________

6. We have more than enough bricks to build the wall. **who?** ____________

   **has?** ____________

7. The bird has a worm in its beak. **what?** ____________

   **has?** ____________

# Subjects and Predicates

**Directions:** Every sentence has two main parts—the subject and the predicate. Draw one line under the subject and two lines under the predicate in each sentence below.

**Example:**

Porcupines are related to mice and rats.

1. They are large rodents.

2. Porcupines have long, sharp quills.

3. The quills stand up straight when it is angry.

4. Most animals stay away from porcupines.

5. Their quills hurt other animals.

6. Porcupines sleep under rocks or bushes.

7. They sleep during the day.

8. Porcupines eat plants at night.

9. North America has some porcupines.

10. They are called New World porcupines.

11. New World porcupines can climb trees.

Name: _____

# Subjects and Predicates

**Directions:** Draw one line under the subjects and two lines under the predicates in the sentences below.

1. My mom likes to plant flowers.

2. Our neighbors walk their dog.

3. Our car needs gas.

4. The children play house.

5. Movies and popcorn go well together.

6. Peanut butter and jelly is my favorite kind of sandwich.

7. Bill, Sue and Nancy ride to the park.

8. We use pencils, markers and pens to write on paper.

9. Trees and shrubs need special care.

Name: _____

# Simple Subjects

A **simple subject** is the main noun or pronoun in the complete subject.

**Directions:** Draw a line between the subject and the predicate. Circle the simple subject.

**Example:** The black (bear)|lives in the zoo.

1. Penguins look like they wear tuxedos.

2. The seal enjoys raw fish.

3. The monkeys like to swing on bars.

4. The beautiful peacock has colorful feathers.

5. Bats like dark places.

6. Some snakes eat small rodents.

7. The orange and brown giraffes have long necks.

8. The baby zebra is close to his mother.

Name: _____

# Compound Subjects

**Compound subjects** are two or more nouns that have the same predicate.

**Directions:** Combine the subjects to create one sentence with a compound subject.

**Example:** Jill can swing.
Whitney can swing.
Luke can swing.

Jill, Whitney and Luke can swing.

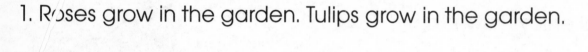

1. Roses grow in the garden. Tulips grow in the garden.

_____

2. Apples are fruit. Oranges are fruit. Bananas are fruit.

_____

3. Bears live in the zoo. Monkeys live in the zoo.

_____

4. Jackets keep us warm. Sweaters keep us warm.

_____

# Compound Subjects

**Directions:** Underline the simple subjects in each compound subject.

**Example:** <u>Dogs</u> and <u>cats</u> are good pets.

1. Blueberries and strawberries are fruit.

2. Jesse, Jake and Hannah like school.

3. Cows, pigs and sheep live on a farm.

4. Boys and girls ride the bus.

5. My family and I took a trip to Duluth.

6. Fruits and vegetables are good for you.

7. Katarina, Lexi and Mandi like to go swimming.

8. Petunias, impatiens, snapdragons and geraniums are all flowers.

9. Coffee, tea and milk are beverages.

10. Dave, Karla and Tami worked on the project together.

# Simple Predicates

A **simple predicate** is the main verb or verbs in the complete predicate.

**Directions:** Draw a line between the complete subject and the complete predicate. Circle the simple predicate.

**Example:** The ripe apples (fell) to the ground.

1. The farmer scattered feed for the chickens.

2. The horses galloped wildly around the corral.

3. The baby chicks were staying warm by the light.

4. The tractor was bailing hay.

5. The silo was full of grain.

6. The cows were being milked.

7. The milk truck drove up to the barn.

8. The rooster woke everyone up.

Name: _____

# Compound Predicates

**Compound predicates** have two or more verbs that have the same subject.

**Directions:** Combine the predicates to create one sentence with a compound predicate.

**Example:** We went to the zoo.
We watched the monkeys.
We went to the zoo and watched the monkeys.

1. Students read their books. Students do their work.

_____

2. Dogs can bark loudly. Dogs can do tricks.

_____

3. The football player caught the ball. The football player ran.

_____

4. My dad sawed wood. My dad stacked wood.

_____

5. My teddy bear is soft. My teddy bear likes to be hugged.

_____

Name: _____

# Compound Predicates

**Directions:** Underline the simple predicates (verbs) in each predicate.

**Example:** The fans <u>clapped</u> and <u>cheered</u> at the game.

1. The coach talks and encourages the team.

2. The cheerleaders jump and yell.

3. The basketball players dribble and shoot the ball.

4. The basketball bounces and hits the backboard.

5. The ball rolls around the rim and goes into the basket.

6. Everyone leaps up and cheers.

7. The team scores and wins!

Name: _____

# Subjects

**Directions:** Use your own words to write the subjects in the sentences below.

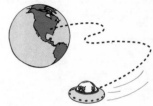

1. _____ landed in my backyard.

2. _____ rushed out of the house.

3. _____ had bright lights.

4. _____ were tall and green.

5. _____ talked to me.

6. _____ came outside with me.

7. _____ ran into the house.

8. _____ shook hands.

9. _____ said funny things.

10. _____ gave us a ride.

11. _____ flew away.

12. _____ will come back soon.

# Predicates

**Directions:** Use your own words to write the predicates in the sentences below.

1. The swimming pool _____ .

2. The water _____ .

3. The sun _____ .

4. I always _____ .

5. My friends _____ .

6. We always _____ .

7. The lifeguard _____ .

8. The rest periods _____ .

9. The lunch _____ .

10. My favorite food _____ .

11. The diving board _____ .

12. We never _____ .

Name: _____

# Review

**Directions:** Use **and** or **but** to make longer, more interesting sentences from two shorter sentences.

1. I have a dog. I have a cat.

_____

2. The sun is shining. The weather is cold.

_____

**Directions:** Draw one line under the subjects in the sentences. Draw two lines under the predicates.

1. We went on a white water rafting trip.

2. Sam and Ben won the best prize.

3. She painted a picture for me.

4. Those flowers are beautiful.

5. She is a great babysitter.

6. My shoes got wet in the creek.

7. The cows are not in the barn.

8. He has a new shirt for the party.

Name: _____

# Word Order

**Word order** is the logical order of words in sentences.

**Directions:** Put the words in order so that each sentence tells a complete idea.

**Example:** outside put cat the

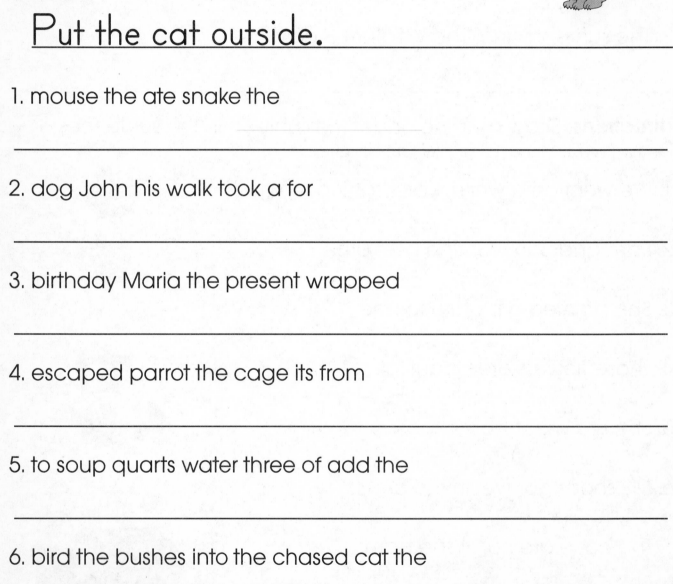

<u>Put the cat outside.</u>_____

1. mouse the ate snake the

   _____

   _____

2. dog John his walk took a for

   _____

3. birthday Maria the present wrapped

   _____

4. escaped parrot the cage its from

   _____

5. to soup quarts water three of add the

   _____

6. bird the bushes into the chased cat the

   _____

Name: _____

# Sentences and Non-Sentences

A **sentence** tells a complete idea.

**Directions:** Circle the groups of words that tell a complete idea.

1. Sharks are fierce hunters.

2. Afraid of sharks.

3. The great white shark will attack people.

4. Other kinds will not.

5. Sharks have an outer row of teeth for grabbing food.

6. When the outer teeth fall out, another row of teeth moves up.

7. Keep the ocean clean by eating dead animals.

8. Not a single bone in its body.

9. Cartilage.

10. Made of the same material as the tip of your nose.

11. Unlike other fish, sharks cannot float.

12. In motion constantly.

13. Even while sleeping.

Name: _____

# Completing a Story

**Directions:** Complete the story, using sentences that tell complete ideas.

One morning, my friend asked me to take my first bus trip

downtown. I was so excited I _____

_____.

At the bus stop, we saw_____. Our bus driver

_____.

When we got off the bus_____

_____. I'd never seen so many

_____.

My favorite part was when we _____

_____.

We stopped to eat _____

_____

_____. I bought a _____

_____.

When we got home, I told my friend, "_____

_____

_____."

Name: _____

# Complete the Sentences

**Directions:** Write your own endings to make the sentences tell a complete idea.

**Example:**

*The Wizard of Oz* is a story about _Dorothy and her dog, Toto_.

1. Dorothy and Toto live on _____.

2. A big storm _____.

3. Dorothy and Toto are carried off to _____.

4. Dorothy meets _____.

5. Dorothy, Toto and their friends follow the _____.

6. Dorothy tries to find _____.

7. The Wizard turns out to be _____.

8. A scary person in the story is _____.

9. The wicked witch is killed by _____.

10. The hot air balloon leaves without _____.

11. Dorothy uses her magic shoes to _____.

Name: _____

# Complete the Sentences

**Directions:** Write your own endings to make the sentences tell a complete idea.

**Example:**

*Cinderella* is a story about ___ Cinderella, her stepmother, stepsisters and the prince. ___

1. Cinderella lives with. _____

2. Her stepmother and her stepsisters _____

3. Cinderella's stepsisters receive _____

4. Cinderella cannot go to the ball because _____

   _____

5. The fairy godmother comes _____

6. The prince dances with _____

7. When the clock strikes midnight, _____

8. The prince's men look for _____

9. The slipper fits _____

10. Cinderella and the prince live _____

Name: _____

# Alliteration

**Alliteration** is the repeated use of beginning sounds. Alliterative sentences are sometimes referred to as tongue twisters.

**Example:**

She sells sea shells by the seashore.
Peter Piper picked a peck of pickled peppers.

**Directions:** Use alliteration to write your own tongue twisters.

1. _____

_____

_____

2. _____

_____

_____

3. _____

_____

_____

# Statements and Questions

**Statements** are sentences that tell about something. Statements begin with a capital letter and end with a period. **Questions** are sentences that ask about something. Questions begin with a capital letter and end with a question mark.

**Directions:** Rewrite the sentences using capital letters and either a period or a question mark.

**Example:** walruses live in the Arctic

_Walruses live in the Arctic._

1. are walruses large sea mammals or fish

_____

2. they spend most of their time in the water and on ice

_____

3. are floating sheets of ice called ice floes

_____

4. are walruses related to seals

_____

5. their skin is thick, wrinkled and almost hairless

_____

# Statements and Questions

**Directions:** Change the statements into questions and the questions into statements.

**Example:**   Jane is happy.          Is Jane happy?
                Were you late?         You were late.

1. The rainbow was brightly colored.

   _____

2. Was the sun coming out?

   _____

3. The dog is doing tricks.

   _____

4. Have you washed the dishes today?

   _____

5. Kurt was the circus ringmaster.

   _____

6. Were you planning on going to thelibrary?

   _____

Name: _____

# Exclamations

**Exclamation points** are used for sentences that express strong feelings. These sentences can have one or two words or be very long.

**Example: Wait!** or **Don't forget to call!**

**Directions:** Add an exclamation point at the end of sentences that express strong feelings. Add a period at the end of the statements.

1. My parents and I were watching television

2. The snow began falling around noon

3. Wow

4. The snow was really coming down

5. We turned the television off and looked out the window

6. The snow looked like a white blanket

7. How beautiful

8. We decided to put on our coats and go outside

9. Hurry

10. Get your sled

11. All the people on the street came out to see the snow

12. How wonderful

13. The children began making a snowman

14. What a great day

Name: _____

# Review

There are three kinds of sentences.

**Statements:** Sentences that tell something. Statements end with a period (**.**).

**Questions:** Sentences that ask a question. Questions end with a question mark (**?**).

**Exclamations:** Sentences that express a strong feeling. Exclamations end with an exclamation point (**!**).

**Directions:** Write what kind of sentence each is.

1. _____ What a super day to go to the zoo!

2. _____ Do you like radishes?

3. _____ I belong to the chess club.

4. _____ Wash the dishes.

5. _____ How much does that cost?

6. _____ Apples grow on trees.

7. _____ Look out the window.

8. _____ Look at the colorful rainbow!

Name: _____

# Contractions

**Contractions** are shortened forms of two words. We use apostrophes to show where letters are missing.

**Example: It is = it's**

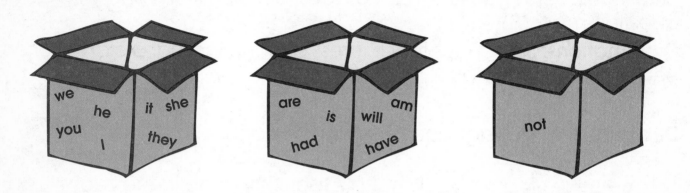

**Directions:** Write the words that are used in each contraction.

we're _____+_____        they'll _____+_____

you'll _____+_____        aren't _____+_____

I'm _____+_____            isn't _____+_____

**Directions:** Write the contraction for the two words shown.

you have _____        have not _____

had not _____          we will _____

they are _____         he is _____

she had _____          it will _____

I am _____              is not _____

---

Name: _____

# Apostrophes

**Apostrophes** are used to show ownership by placing an **s** at the end of a single person, place or thing.

**Example:** Mary**'s** cat

**Directions:** Write the apostrophes in the contractions below.

**Example:** We shouldn' t be going to their house so late at night.

1. We didn t think that the ice cream would melt so fast.

2. They re never around when we re ready to go.

3. Didn t you need to make a phone call?

4. Who s going to help you paint the bicycle red?

**Directions:** Add an apostrophe and an **s** to the words to show ownership of a person, place or thing.

**Example:** Jill**'s** bike is broken.

1. That is Holly   flower garden.

2. Mark   new skates are black and green.

3. Mom threw away Dad   old shoes.

4. Buster   food dish was lost in the snowstorm.

# Quotation Marks

**Quotation marks** are punctuation marks that tell what is said by a person. Quotation marks go before the first word and after the punctuation of a direct quote. The first word of a direct quote begins with a capital letter.

**Example:** Katie said, "Never go in the water without a friend."

**Directions:** Put quotation marks around the correct words in the sentences below.

**Example**: "Wait for me, please," said Laura.

1. John, would you like to visit a jungle? asked his uncle.

2. The police officer said, Don't worry, we'll help you.

3. James shouted, Hit a home run!

4. My friend Carol said, I really don't like cheeseburgers.

---

**Directions:** Write your own quotations by answering the questions below. Be sure to put quotation marks around your words.

1. What would you say if you saw a dinosaur?

   _____

   _____

2. What would your best friend say if your hair turned purple?

   _____

   _____

Name: _____

# Quotation Marks

**Directions:** Put quotation marks around the correct words in the sentences below.

1. Can we go for a bike ride? asked Katrina.

_____

2. Yes, said Mom.

_____

3. Let's go to the park, said Mike.

_____

4. Great idea! said Mom.

_____

5. How long until we get there? asked Katrina.

_____

6. Soon, said Mike.

_____

7. Here we are! exclaimed Mom.

_____

Name: _____

# Review

**Directions:** Unscramble this sentence and write it on the line below.

1. have tails short bodies wide and pigs

_____

**Directions:** Put a question mark, a period or an exclamation point at the end of the following sentences:

1. Tiny pigs, called miniature pigs, weigh only 60 pounds

2. Pigs can weigh as much as 800 pounds

3. Wow

4. Do pigs have spots

**Directions:** Put the apostrophes in the sentences to replace a letter or to show ownership.

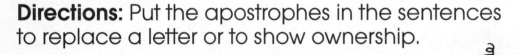

1. A pig s pen should have water in it.

2. They re really not animals that like mud.

3. It s an animal that needs water to keep cool.

4. Most farmers don t give them their own pools.

**Directions:** Put quotation marks in the sentences below.

1. You eat like a pig, said my Uncle Homer.

2. That is not an insult, I told him.

3. Pigs are really clean animals, I said.

Name: _____

# Acronyms

An **acronym** is a word formed by the first letters of each word.

**Example:** SCUBA

        **S**elf **C**ontained **U**nderwater **B**reathing **A**pparatus

**Directions:** List other acronyms you know.

   **VIP**      Very important person _____

  **DARE**   Drug Abuse Resistance Education _____

_____        _____

_____        _____

_____        _____

_____        _____

_____        _____

_____        _____

_____        _____

# Parts of a Paragraph

A **paragraph** is a group of sentences that all tell about the same thing. Most paragraphs have three parts: a **beginning**, a **middle** and an **end**.

**Directions:** Write **beginning**, **middle** or **end** next to each sentence in the scrambled paragraphs below. There can be more than one middle sentence.

**Example:**

_____middle_____ We took the tire off the car.

___beginning___ On the way to Aunt Louise's, we had a flat tire.

_____middle_____ We patched the hole in the tire.

_____end_____ We put the tire on and started driving again.

_____ I took all the ingredients out of the cupboard.

_____ One morning, I decided to bake a pumpkin pie.

_____ I forgot to add the pumpkin!

_____ I mixed the ingredients together, but something was missing.

_____ The sun was very hot and our throats were dry.

_____ We finally decided to turn back.

_____ We started our hike very early in the morning.

_____ It kept getting hotter as we walked.

Name: _____

# Topic Sentences

A **topic sentence** is usually the first sentence in a paragraph. It tells what the story will be about.

**Directions:** Read the following sentences. Circle the topic sentence that should go first in the paragraph that follows.

Rainbows have seven colors.

There's a pot of gold.

I like rainbows.

The colors are red, orange, yellow, green, blue, indigo and violet. Red forms the outer edge, with violet on the inside of the rainbow.

_____

He cut down a cherry tree.

His wife was named Martha.

George Washington was a good president.

He helped our country get started. He chose intelligent leaders to help him run the country.

_____

Mark Twain was a great author.

Mark Twain was unhappy sometimes.

Mark Twain was born in Missouri.

One of his most famous books is *Huckleberry Finn*. He wrote many other great books.

ENGLISH 3

# Middle Sentences

**Middle sentences** support the topic sentence. They tell more about it.

**Directions:** Underline the middle sentences that support each topic sentence below.

**Topic Sentence:**

Penguins are birds that cannot fly.

Pelicans can spear fish with their sharp bills.

Many penguins waddle or hop about on land.

Even though they cannot fly, they are excellent swimmers.

Pelicans keep their food in a pouch.

**Topic Sentence:**

Volleyball is a team sport in which the players hit the ball over the net.

There are two teams with six players on each team.

My friend John would rather play tennis with Lisa.

Players can use their heads or their hands.

I broke my hand once playing handball.

**Topic Sentence:**

Pikes Peak is the most famous of all the Rocky Mountains.

Some mountains have more trees than other mountains.

Many people like to climb to the top.

Many people like to ski and camp there, too.

The weather is colder at the top of most mountains.

# Ending Sentences

**Ending sentences** are sentences that tie the story together.

**Directions:** Choose the correct ending sentence for each story from the sentences below. Write it at the end of the paragraph.

A new pair of shoes!
All the corn on the cob I could eat!
A new eraser!

### Corn on the Cob

Corn on the cob used to be my favorite food. That is, until I lost my four front teeth. For one whole year, I had to sit and watch everyone else eat my favorite food without me. Mom gave me creamed corn, but it just wasn't the same. When my teeth finally came in, Dad said he had a surprise for me. I thought I was going to get a bike or a new C.D. player or something. I was just as happy to get what I did.

I would like to take a train ride every year.
Trains move faster than I thought they would.
She had brought her new gerbil along for the ride.

### A Train Ride

When our family took its first train ride, my sister brought along a big box. She would not tell anyone what she had in it. In the middle of the trip, we heard a sound coming from the box. "Okay, Jan, now you have to open the box," said Mom. When she opened the box we were surprised.

Name: _____

# Review

**Directions:** Write your own story with a topic sentence, at least three middle sentences and an ending sentence. Use your own idea or use one of these ideas for a story title:

The Best Day I Ever Had
My First Pet
I Was So Unhappy I Cried

If I Could Do Anything
My Best Friend
Why I Like Myself

Title:

_____

Topic Sentence:

_____

Middle Sentences:

_____

_____

_____

Ending Sentence:

_____

# Letter Writing

**Letters** have five parts: the **heading**, the **greeting**, the **body**, the **closing** and the **signature**.

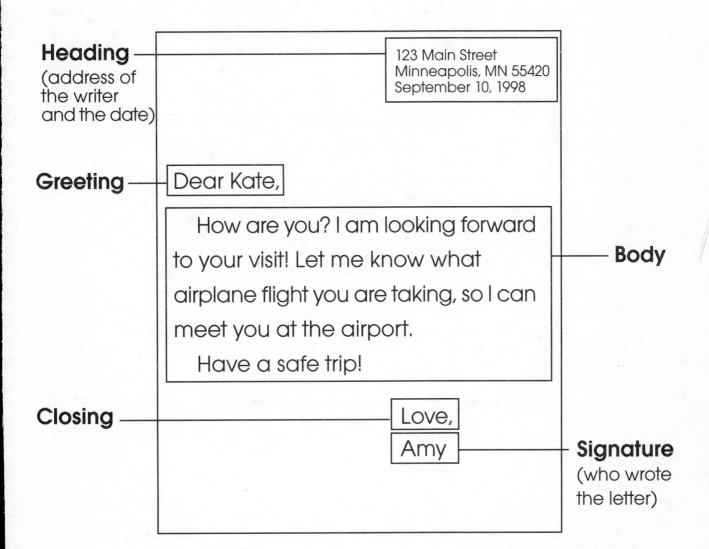

**Heading**
(address of
the writer
and the date)

123 Main Street
Minneapolis, MN 55420
September 10, 1998

**Greeting**

Dear Kate,

How are you? I am looking forward to your visit! Let me know what airplane flight you are taking, so I can meet you at the airport.

Have a safe trip!

**Body**

**Closing**

Love,

Amy

**Signature**
(who wrote
the letter)

# Letter Writing

**Directions:** Write a friendly letter below. Be sure to include a heading, greeting, body, closing and signature.

_____

_____

_____
(heading)

_____, 
(greeting)

_____

_____

(body) _____

_____

_____

_____, (closing)

_____ (signature)

Name: _____

# Poetry

**Haiku** is a form of Japanese poetry which is often about nature. There are 3 lines: 5 syllables, 7 syllables, 5 syllables.

**Example:**

| | |
|---|---|
| The rain falls softly, | 5 |
| Touching the leaves on the trees, | 7 |
| Bathing tenderly. | 5 |

**Directions:** Choose a topic in nature that would make a good haiku. Think of words to describe your topic. Write and illustrate your haiku below.

_____

_____

_____

Name: _____

# Poetry

**Shape poems** are words that form the shape of the thing being written about.

**Example:**

**Directions:** Create your own shape poem below.

# Glossary

**Abbreviations:** A shortened form of a word. Most abbreviations begin with a capital letter and end with a period. Example: Doctor = **Dr.**

**Acronyms:** A word that is formed by the first letters of each word. Example: **DARE** (Drug Abuse Resistance Education).

**Adjectives:** Words that tell more about a person, place or thing. Example: **sad.**

**Adverbs:** Words that describe verbs. Abverbs tell where, how and when. Examples: **quickly, now.**

**Alliteration:** The repeated use of beginning sounds. They are also known as tongue twisters. Example: **P**eter **P**iper **p**icked a **p**eck of **p**ickled **p**eppers.

**Alphabetical Order:** Putting letters or words in the order in which they appear in the alphabet.

**Antonyms:** Words that are opposites. Example: **big** and **small** are antonyms.

**Apostrophes:** Punctuation that is used with contractions in place of the missing letter or used to show ownership. Examples: **don't, Susan's.**

**Articles:** Small words that help us better understand nouns. Example: **a, an.**

**Capitalization:** Letters that are used at the beginning of names of people, places, days, months and holidays. Capital letters are also used at the beginning of sentences.

**Commas:** Punctuation marks which are used to separate words or phrases. They are also used to separate dates from years, cities from states, etc.

**Common Nouns:** Nouns that name any member of a group of people, places or things rather than specific people, places or things. Example: **person.**

**Compound Predicates:** Two or more verbs that have the same subject.

**Compound Sentences:** Two complete ideas that are joined together into one sentence by a conjunction.

**Compound Subjects:** Two or more nouns that have the same predicate.

**Compound Words:** Two words that are put together to make one new word. Example: **base** + **ball** = **baseball.**

**Contractions:** A short way to write two words together. Example: **it is** = **it's.**

**Ending Sentences:** Sentences at the end of a paragraph that tie the story together.

**Exclamations:** Sentences that express strong feelings. Exclamations often end with an exclamation point. These sentences can be short or long, and can be a command. Example: **Look at that!**

**Future-Tense Verbs:** A verb that tells about something that has not happened yet but will happen in the future. Will or shall are usually used with future tense. Example: We **will eat** soon.

**Haiku:** A Japanese form of poetry. Most have 5 syllables in the first and third lines and 7 syllables in the middle line.

**Helping Verbs:** A word used with an action verb. Example: They **are** helping.

**Homophones:** Words that sound the same but are spelled differently and mean different things. Example: **blue** and **blew**.

**Irregular Verbs:** Verbs that do not change from the present tense to the past tense in the regular way with **d** or **ed**. Example: **run**, ran.

**Linking Verbs:** Verbs that connect the noun to a descriptive word. Linking verbs are always a form of "to be." Example: I **am** tired.

**Middle Sentences:** Sentences that support the topic sentence in a paragraph.

**Nouns:** Words that name a person, place or thing.

**Paragraph:** A group of sentences that all tell about the same thing.

**Past-Tense Verbs:** A verb that tells about something that has already happened. A **d** or **ed** is usually added to the end of the word. Example: **walked**.

**Plural Nouns:** Nouns which name more than one person, place or thing.

**Possessive Nouns:** Nouns that tell who or what is the owner of something. Example: the **dog's** ball.

**Possessive Pronouns:** Pronouns that show ownership. Example: **his** dish.

**Predicates:** The verb in the sentence that tells the main action. It tell what the subject is doing, has done or will do.

**Prefixes:** Special word parts added to the beginnings of words. Prefixes change the meaning of words. Example: **re**do.

**Prepositions:** Words that show the relationship between a noun or pronoun and another word in the sentence. Example: The boy is **behind** the chair.

**Present-Tense Verbs:** A verb that tells about something that is happening now, happens often or is about to happen. An **s** or **ing** is usually added to the verb. Examples: **sings, singing**.

**Pronouns:** Words that can be used in place of nouns. Example: **It**.

**Proper Nouns:** Names of specific people, places or things. Example: **Iowa**.

**Questions:** Sentences that ask. They begin with a capital letter and end with a question mark.

**Quotations Marks:** Punctuation marks that tell what is said by a person. Quotation marks go before and after a direct quote. Example: She said, "Here I am!"

**Sentences:** Sentences tell a complete idea with a noun and a verb. They begin with a capital letter and have end punctuation (a period, question mark or exclamation point).

**Simple Predicates:** The main verb of the predicate part of the sentence.
Example: Dad will **cook** for us tonight.

**Simple Subjects:** The main noun in the complete subject part of the sentence.
Example: The silly **boy** ran around.

**Statements:** A sentence which tells something. Statements begin with a capital letter and end with a period.

**Subjects:** The noun that does the action. It tells who or what the sentence is about. A noun or pronoun will always be part of the subject.

**Suffixes:** Word parts added to the end of words. Suffixes change the meaning of words. Example: care**less**.

**Synonyms:** Words that mean the same or nearly the same. Example: **small** and **little**.

**Topic Sentence:** Usually the first sentence in a paragraph. The topic sentence tells what the story is about.

**Verbs:** The action words in a sentence. The word that tells what something does or that something exists. Example: **run, is.**

**Vowels:** The letters **a, e, i, o** and **u**.

**Word Order:** The logical order of words in a sentence.

# Answer Key

---

## Alphabetical Order

**Directions: Alphabetical order** is putting words in the order in which they appear in the alphabet. Put the eggs in alphabetical order. The first and last words are done for you.

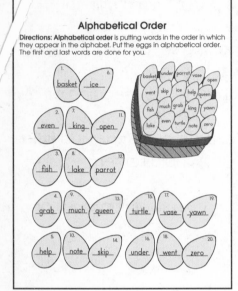

1. basket
2. even
3. fish
4. grab
5. help
6. ice
7. king
8. lake
9. much
10. note
11. open
12. parrot
13. queen
14. skip
15. turtle
16. under
17. vase
18. went
19. yawn
20. zero

---

## Alphabetical Order

**Directions:** Write the words in alphabetical order. Look at the first letter of each word. If the first letter of two words is the same, look at the second letter.

**Example:** l@mp    Lamp comes first because
l(i)ght    **a** comes before **i** in the alphabet.

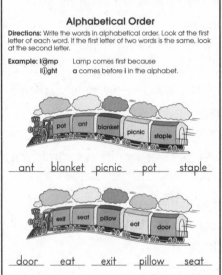

ant    blanket    picnic    pot    staple

door    eat    exit    pillow    seat

---

## Alphabetical Order

Arrange the words in alphabetical order by the first and second letters.

**Directions:** Read the words and circle the first letter of each word. Then write the words in alphabetical order on the bricks below.

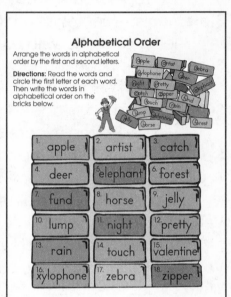

1. apple
2. artist
3. catch
4. deer
5. elephant
6. forest
7. fund
8. horse
9. jelly
10. lump
11. night
12. pretty
13. rain
14. touch
15. valentine
16. xylophone
17. zebra
18. zipper

**3**      **4**      **5**

---

## Compound Words

**Compound words** are two words that are put together to make one new word.
**Example:**

nut + shell = nutshell

**Directions:** Choose a word from the box to make compound words in the sentences below.

| board | bone | ground | prints | shake | house |
| brush | man | top | shell | ball | hive |

**Example:**
The bird built its nest in the **treetop**.

1. We pitched our tent at the camp <u>ground</u>.
2. You would not be able to stand up without your back <u>bone</u>.
3. The police officer looked for finger <u>prints</u>.
4. She placed the hair <u>brush</u> in her purse.
5. It is important to have a firm hand <u>shake</u>.
6. The teacher wrote on the chalk <u>board</u>.
7. The egg <u>shell</u> is cracked.
8. Our whole family plays foot <u>ball</u> together.
9. Be sure to put a top hat on the snow <u>man</u>.
10. Spot never sleeps in his dog <u>house</u>.
11. The beekeeper must check the bee <u>hive</u> today.

---

## Compound Words

**Directions:** Write your own compound words by mixing up the words below. Add and subtract parts of each compound word to make up fun new compound words. Then draw pictures to illustrate your new words!

**Examples:**    rattlesnake + starfish = rattlefish
           junkyard + scarecrow = junkcrow

| horseshoe | bedroom | moonlight | scarecrow |
| spaceship | seaweed | goldfish | mailbox |
| butterfly  | farmhouse | sailboat  | bodyguard |
| sunshine  | sidewalk | lifeguard | junkyard |

*Answers will vary.*

---

## Antonyms

**Antonyms** are words that are opposites.

**Example:**    hairy      bald

**Directions:** Choose a word from the box to complete each sentence below.

| open | right | light | full | late | below |
| hard | clean | slow | quiet | old | nice |

**Example:**
My car was dirty, but now it's **clean**.

1. Sometimes my cat is naughty, and sometimes she's <u>nice</u>.
2. The sign said, "Closed," but the door was <u>open</u>.
3. Is the glass half empty or half <u>full</u>?
4. I bought new shoes, but I like my <u>old</u> ones better.
5. Skating is easy for me, but <u>hard</u> for my brother.
6. The sky is dark at night and <u>light</u> during the day.
7. I like a noisy house, but my mother likes a <u>quiet</u> one.
8. My friend says I'm wrong, but I say I'm <u>right</u>.
9. Jason is a fast runner, but Adam is a <u>slow</u> runner.
10. We were supposed to be early, but we were <u>late</u>.

**6**      **7**      **8**

---

## Antonyms

**Directions:** Write the antonym pairs from each sentence in the boxes.

**Example:** Many things are bought and sold at the market.

| bought | sold |
|---|---|

1. I thought I lost my dog, but someone found him.

| lost | found |
|---|---|

2. The teacher will ask questions for the students to answer.

| ask | answer |
|---|---|

3. Airplanes arrive and depart from the airport.

| arrive | depart |
|---|---|

4. The water in the pool was cold compared to the warm water in the whirlpool.

| cold | warm |
|---|---|

5. The tortoise was slow, but the hare was fast.

| slow | fast |
|---|---|

**9**

## Synonyms

**Synonyms** are words that mean almost the same thing.

**Example: small** and **little**

**Directions:** Look at the clues below. Complete the puzzle with words from the box that mean the same thing.

| pot | pretty | late | huge | close |
|---|---|---|---|---|
| funny | smile | fast | unhappy | exit |

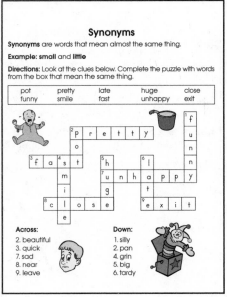

**Across:**
2. beautiful
3. quick
7. sad
8. near
9. leave

**Down:**
1. silly
2. pan
4. grin
5. big
6. tardy

**10**

## Synonyms

**Directions:** Match the pairs of synonyms.

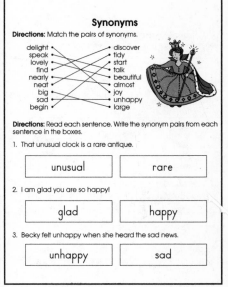

delight — discover
speak — tidy
lovely — start
find — talk
nearly — beautiful
neat — almost
big — joy
sad — unhappy
begin — large

**Directions:** Read each sentence. Write the synonym pairs from each sentence in the boxes.

1. That unusual clock is a rare antique.

| unusual | rare |
|---|---|

2. I am glad you are so happy!

| glad | happy |
|---|---|

3. Becky felt unhappy when she heard the sad news.

| unhappy | sad |
|---|---|

**11**

## Homophones

**Homophones** are words that sound the same but are spelled differently and have different meanings.

**Example:**

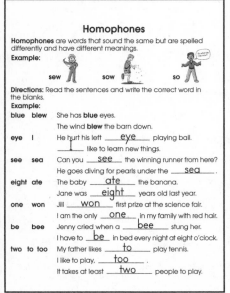

**Directions:** Read the sentences and write the correct word in the blanks.

**Example:**

| blue blew | She has **blue** eyes. |
|---|---|
| | The wind **blew** the barn down. |
| eye I | He hurt his left ___eye___ playing ball. |
| | ___I___ like to learn new things. |
| see sea | Can you ___see___ the winning runner from here? |
| | He goes diving for pearls under the ___sea___. |
| eight ate | The baby ___ate___ the banana. |
| | Jane was ___eight___ years old last year. |
| one won | Jill ___won___ first prize at the science fair. |
| | I am the only ___one___ in my family with red hair. |
| be bee | Jenny cried when a ___bee___ stung her. |
| | I have to ___be___ in bed every night at eight o'clock. |
| two to too | My father likes ___to___ play tennis. |
| | I like to play, ___too___. |
| | It takes at least ___two___ people to play. |

**12**

## Homophones

**Directions:** Read the clues below. Use the box to help you write the correct words in the puzzle.

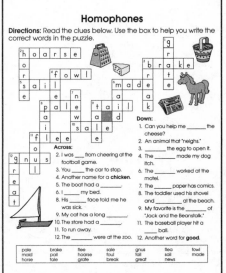

**Across:**
2. I was ___ from cheering at the football game.
3. You ___ the car to stop.
4. Another name for a **chicken**.
5. The boat had a ___.
6. I ___ my bed.
8. His ___ face told me he was sick.
9. My cat has a long ___.
10. The store had a ___.
11. To run away.
12. The ___ were at the zoo.

**Down:**
1. Can you help me ___ the cheese?
2. An animal that "neighs."
3. ___ the egg to open it.
4. The ___ made my dog itch.
6. The ___ worked at the motel.
7. The ___ paper has comics.
8. The toddler used his shovel and ___ at the beach.
9. My favorite is the ___ of "Jack and the Beanstalk."
11. The baseball player hit a ___ ball.
12. Another word for **good**.

| pale | brake | flee | sale | gnus | flea | fowl |
|---|---|---|---|---|---|---|
| maid | pail | hoarse | foul | tail | sail | made |
| horse | tale | grate | break | great | news | |

**13**

## Review

**Directions:** Write the correct word to complete the sentences below.

| Their There | ___Their___ suitcases were lost at the airport. |
|---|---|
| ant aunt | My ___aunt___ and uncle are coming to visit. |
| sale sail | My brother is learning to ___sail___. |
| nose knows | Jenny ___knows___ how to play a violin. |
| pair pear | She put a ripe ___pear___ in my lunchbox. |
| Gentle Early | ___Gentle___ means the same as **tame**. |
| below apart | The opposite of **above** is ___below___. |
| Correct Wet | ___Correct___ means the same as **right**. |
| Little Dry | ___Little___ means the same as **small**. |
| Wrong Quick | ___Quick___ means the same as **fast**. |
| late off | The opposite of **on** is ___off___. |
| under around | The opposite of **over** is ___under___. |

Now, circle the first letter of each word you wrote above. Write the words in alphabetical order on the lines below.

1. ___aunt___
2. ___below___
3. ___Correct___
4. ___Gentle___
5. ___knows___
6. ___Little___
7. ___off___
8. ___pear___
9. ___Quick___
10. ___sail___
11. ___Their___
12. ___under___

**14**

## Nouns

**Nouns** are words that tell the names of people, places or things.

**Directions:** Read the words below. Then write them in the correct column.

| | | |
|---|---|---|
| goat | Mrs. Jackson | girl |
| beach | tree | song |
| mouth | park | Jean Rivers |
| finger | flower | New York |
| Kevin Jones | Elm City | Frank Gates |
| Main Street | theater | skates |
| River Park | father | boy |

**Person**

**Place**

**Thing**

| Person | Place | Thing |
|---|---|---|
| Kevin Jones | beach | goat |
| Mrs. Jackson | Main Street | mouth |
| father | River Park | finger |
| girl | park | tree |
| Jean Rivers | Elm City | flower |
| Frank Gates | theater | song |
| boy | New York | skates |

**15**

## Nouns

Nouns can also name ideas. **Ideas** are things we cannot see or touch such as bravery, beauty or honesty.

**Directions:** Underline the "idea" nouns in each sentence.

1. Respect is something that must be earned.

2. Truth and justice are two things that are highly valued.

3. The beauty of the flower garden was breathtaking.

4. Skills must be learned in order to master new things.

5. His courage impressed everyone.

**16**

## Common Nouns

**Common nouns** are nouns that name any member of a group of people, places or things, rather than specific people, places or things.

**Directions:** Read the sentences below and write the common noun found in each sentence.

**Example:** ___socks___ My socks do not match.

1. ___bird___ The bird could not fly.
2. ___jelly beans___ Ben likes to eat jelly beans.
3. ___mother___ I am going to meet my mother.
4. ___lake___ We will go swimming in the lake tomorrow.
5. ___flowers___ I hope the flowers will grow quickly.
6. ___eggs___ We colored eggs together.
7. ___bicycle___ It is easy to ride a bicycle.
8. ___cousin___ My cousin is very tall.
9. ___boat___ Ted and Jane went fishing in their boat.
10. ___prize___ They won a prize yesterday.
11. ___ankle___ She fell down and twisted her ankle.
12. ___brother___ My brother was born today.
13. ___slide___ She went down the slide.
14. ___doctor___ Ray went to the doctor today.

**17**

## Proper Nouns

**Proper nouns** are names of specific people, places or things. Proper nouns begin with a capital letter.

**Directions:** Read the sentences below and circle the proper nouns found in each sentence.

**Example:** (Aunt Frances) gave me a puppy for my birthday.

1. We lived on (Jackson Street) before we moved to our new house.
2. (Angela's) birthday party is tomorrow night.
3. We drove through (Cheyenne, Wyoming) on our way home.
4. (Dr. Charles) always gives me a treat for not crying.
5. (George Washington) was our first president.
6. Our class took a field trip to the (Johnson Flower Farm.)
7. (Uncle Jack) lives in (New York City.)
8. (Amy) and (Elizabeth) are best friends.
9. We buy doughnuts at the (Grayson Bakery.)
10. My favorite movie is (E.T.)
11. We flew to (Miami, Florida) in a plane.
12. We go to (Riverfront Stadium) to watch the baseball games.
13. (Mr. Fields) is a wonderful music teacher.
14. My best friend is (Tom Dunlap.)

**18**

## Proper Nouns

**Directions:** Rewrite each sentence, capitalizing the proper nouns.

1. mike's birthday is in september.

Mike's birthday is in September.

2. aunt katie lives in detroit, michigan.

Aunt Katie lives in Detroit, Michigan.

3. in july, we went to canada.

In July, we went to Canada.

4. kathy jones moved to utah in january.

Kathy Jones moved to Utah in January.

5. My favorite holiday is valentine's day in february.

My favorite holiday is Valentine's Day in February.

6. On friday, mr. polzin gave the smith family a tour.

On Friday, Mr. Polzin gave the Smith family a tour.

7. saturday, uncle cliff and I will go to the mall of america in minnesota.

Saturday, Uncle Cliff and I will go to the Mall of America in Minnesota.

**19**

## Proper Nouns

**Directions:** Write about you! Write a proper noun for each category below. Capitalize the first letter of each proper noun.

1. Your first name: _____

2. Your last name: _____

3. Your street: _____

4. Your city: _____

5. Your state: _____

6. Your school: _____

7. Your best friend's name: _____

8. Your teacher: _____

9. Your favorite book character: _____

10. Your favorite vacation place: _____

*Answers will vary.*

**20**

## Common and Proper Nouns

**Directions:** Look at the list of nouns in the box. Write the common nouns under the kite. Write the proper nouns under the balloon. Remember to capitalize the first letter of each proper noun.

| lisa smith |
| cats |
| shoelace |
| saturday |
| dr. martin |
| whistle |
| teddy bears |
| main street |
| may |
| boy |
| lawn chair |
| mary stewart |
| bird |
| florida |
| school |
| apples |
| washington, d.c. |
| pine cone |
| elizabeth jones |
| charley reynolds |

cats     Lisa Smith
shoelace     Saturday
whistle     Dr. Martin
teddy bears     Main Street
boy     Mary Stewart
lawn chair     Florida
bird     Washington, D.C.
school     May
apples     Elizabeth Jones
pine cone     Charley Reynolds

**21**

## Plural Nouns

A **plural** is more than one person, place or thing. We usually add an **s** to show that a noun names more than one. If a noun ends in **x, ch, sh** or **s**, we add an **es** to the word.

**Example:** pizza     pizzas

**Directions:** Write the plural of the words below.

**Example: dog + s = dogs**

| cat | cats |
| boot | boots |
| house | houses |

**Example: ax + es = axes**

| fox | foxes |
| tax | taxes |
| box | boxes |

**Example: dish + es = dishes**

| bush | bushes |
| ash | ashes |
| brush | brushes |

**Example: peach + es = peaches**

| lunch | lunches |
| bunch | bunches |
| punch | punches |

**Example: glass + es = glasses**

| mess | messes |
| guess | guesses |
| class | classes |

walrus

walruses

**22**

## Plural Nouns

To write the plural forms of words ending in **y**, we change the **y** to **ie** and add **s**.

**Example:** pony     ponies

**Directions:** Write the plural of each noun on the lines below.

| berry | berries |
| cherry | cherries |
| bunny | bunnies |
| penny | pennies |
| family | families |
| candy | candies |
| party | parties |

Now, write a story using some of the words that end in **y**. Remember to use capital letters and periods.

_Answers will vary._

**23**

## Plural Nouns

**Directions:** Write the plural of each noun to complete the sentences below. Remember to change the **y** to **ie** before you add **s**!

1. I am going to two birthday ___parties___ this week.
(party)

2. Sandy picked some ___cherries___ for Mom's pie.
(cherry)

3. At the store, we saw lots of ___bunnies___.
(bunny)

4. My change at the candy store was three ___pennies___.
(penny)

5. All the ___ladies___ baked cookies for the bake sale.
(lady)

6. Thanksgiving is a special time for ___families___ to gather together.
(family)

7. Boston and New York are very large ___cities___.
(city)

**24**

## Plural Nouns

Some words have special plural forms.

**Example:** leaf     leaves

| tooth | teeth |
| child | children |
| foot | feet |
| mouse | mice |
| woman | women |
| man | men |

**Directions:** Some of the words in the box are special plurals. Complete each sentence with a plural from the box. Then write the letters from the boxes in the blanks below to solve the puzzle.

1. I lost my two front t e e t h !

2. My sister has two pet m i c e .

3. Her favorite book is Little W o m e n .

4. The circus clown had big f e e t .

5. The teacher played a game with the c h i l d r e n .

Take good care of this pearly plural!

t e e t h
1   2   3   4   5

**25**

## Plural Nouns

**Directions:** The **singular form** of a word shows one person, place or thing. Write the singular form of each noun on the lines below.

| cherries | cherry |
| lunches | lunch |
| countries | country |
| leaves | leaf |
| churches | church |
| arms | arm |
| boxes | box |
| men | man |
| wheels | wheel |
| pictures | picture |
| cities | city |
| places | place |
| ostriches | ostrich |
| glasses | glass |

**26**

## Review

**Directions:** Circle the common nouns in each sentence. Underline the proper nouns. Then write the plural form of each common noun on the lines below.

**What would you take on a space ship?**

1. Jason will take his bicycle and his radio.
2. Lauren says she cannot live without her pet.
3. Max will take his lunch.
4. Charlie and Greg are taking a game and a television.
5. Katie wants to take the entire city of Nashville, Tennessee.
6. Jack's mother said he could take his messy room with him.
7. Andy wants his teacher Mr. Temple to go with him.
8. Jessica wants to take a neighbor from Mulberry Street.
9. Jill likes to swim and is taking the Metro City Pool with her.
10. I think I am going to take my dog, Mr. Buster, with me.

bicycles
radios
pets
lunches          cities          teachers
games           mothers        neighbors
televisions       rooms           dogs

**27**

## Possessive Nouns

**Possessive nouns** tell who or what is the owner of something. With singular nouns, we use an apostrophe **before** the **s**. With plural nouns, we use an apostrophe **after** the **s**.

**Example:**
singular: one elephant
The **elephant's** dance was wonderful.
plural: more than one elephant
The **elephants'** dance was wonderful.

**Directions:** Put the apostrophe in the correct place in each bold word. Then write the word in the blank.

1. The **lions** cage was big. _lion's or lions'_
2. The **bears** costumes were purple. _bears'_
3. One **boys** laughter was very loud. _boy's_
4. The **trainers** dogs were dancing about. _trainer's or trainers'_
5. The **mans** popcorn was tasty and good. _man's_
6. **Marks** cotton candy was delicious. _Mark's_
7. A little **girls** balloon burst in the air. _girl's_
8. The big **clowns** tricks were very funny. _clown's or clowns'_
9. **Lauras** sister clapped for the clowns. _Laura's_
10. The **womans** money was lost in the crowd. _woman's_
11. **Kellys** mother picked her up early. _Kelly's_

**28**

## Possessive Nouns

**Directions:** Circle the correct possessive noun in each sentence and write it in the blank.

**Example:** One _girl's_ mother is a teacher.
(girl's) girls'

1. The _cat's_ tail is long.
(cat's) cats'
2. One _boy's_ baseball bat is aluminum.
(boy's) boys'
3. A _waitresses'_ aprons are white.
(waitresses') waitress's
4. My _grandmother's_ apple pie is the best!
(grandmother's) grandmothers'
5. My five _brothers'_ uniforms are dirty.
brother's (brothers')
6. The _child's_ doll is pretty.
(child's) childs'
7. This _dogs'_ collars are different colors.
dog's (dogs')
8. The _cow's_ tail is short.
(cow's) cows'

**29**

## Pronouns

**Pronouns** are words that are used in place of nouns.
**Examples:** he, she, it, they, him, them, her, him

**Directions:** Read each sentence. Write the pronoun that takes the place of each noun.

**Example:**
The **monkey** dropped the banana. _It_

1. **Dad** washed the car last night. _He_
2. **Mary and David** took a walk in the park. _They_
3. **Peggy** spent the night at her grandmother's house. _She_
4. The baseball **players** lost their game. _they_
5. **Mike Van Meter** is a great soccer player. _He_
6. The **parrot** can say five different words. _It_
7. **Megan** wrote a story in class today. _She_
8. They gave a party for **Teresa**. _her_
9. Everyone in the class was happy for **Ted**. _him_
10. The children petted the **giraffe**. _it_
11. Linda put the **kittens** near the warm stove. _them_
12. **Gina** made a chocolate cake for my birthday. _She_
13. **Pete and Matt** played baseball on the same team. _They_
14. Give the books to **Herbie**. _him_

**30**

## Pronouns

| Singular Pronouns | Plural Pronouns |
| --- | --- |
| I me my mine | we us our ours |
| you your yours | you your yours |
| he she it her | they them their theirs |
| hers his its him | |

**Directions:** Underline the pronouns in each sentence.

1. Mom told _us_ to wash _our_ hands.
2. Did _you_ go to the store?
3. _We_ should buy _him_ a present.
4. _I_ called _you_ about _their_ party.
5. _Our_ house had damage on _its_ roof.
6. _They_ want to give _you_ a prize at _our_ party.
7. _My_ cat ate _her_ sandwich.
8. _Your_ coat looks like _his_ coat.

**31**

## Pronouns

We use the pronouns **I** and **we** when talking about the person or people doing the action.

**Example: I** can roller skate. **We** can roller skate.

We use **me** and **us** when talking about something that is happening to a person or people.

**Example:** They gave **me** the roller skates.
They gave **us** the roller skates.

**Directions:** Circle the correct pronoun and write it in the blank.

**Example:**
_We_ are going to the picnic together. (We) Us

1. _I_ am finished with my science project. (I) Me
2. Eric passed the football to _me_. (me) I
3. They ate dinner with _us_ last night. we (us)
4. _I_ like spinach better than ice cream. (I) Me
5. Mom came in the room to tell _me_ good night. (me) I
6. _We_ had a pizza party in my backyard. Us (We)
7. They told _us_ the good news. (us) we
8. Tom and _I_ went to the store. me (I)
9. She is taking _me_ with her to the movies. I (me)
10. Katie and _I_ are good friends. (I) me

**32**

## Possessive Pronouns

**Possessive pronouns** show ownership.
**Example:** **his** hat, **her** shoes, **our** dog
We can use these pronouns before a noun:
**my, our, you, his, her, its, their**
**Example:** That is **my** bike.
We can use these pronouns on their own:
**mine, yours, ours, his, hers, theirs, its**
**Example:** That is **mine.**
**Directions:** Write each sentence again, using a pronoun instead of the words in bold letters. Be sure to use capitals and periods.
**Example:**

My **dog's** bowl is brown.　　**Its** bowl is brown.

1. That is **Lisa's** book.　　That is her book.

2. This is **my** pencil.　　This is mine.

3. This hat is **your** hat.　　This hat is yours.

4. Fifi is **Kevin's** cat.　　Fifi is his cat.

5. That beautiful house is **our** home.
That beautiful house is ours.

6. **The gerbil's** cage is too small.
Its cage is too small.

**33**

## Abbreviations

An **abbreviation** is the shortened form of a word. Most abbreviations begin with a capital letter and end with a period.

| | | | |
|---|---|---|---|
| Mr. | Mister | St. | Street |
| Mrs. | Missus | Ave. | Avenue |
| Dr. | Doctor | Blvd. | Boulevard |
| A.M. | before noon | Rd. | Road |
| P.M. | after noon | | |

Days of the week: Sun. Mon. Tues. Wed. Thurs. Fri. Sat.
Months of the year: Jan. Feb. Mar. Apr. Aug. Sept. Oct. Nov. Dec.

**Directions:** Write the abbreviations for each word.

| | | | | | |
|---|---|---|---|---|---|
| street | St. | doctor | Dr. | Tuesday | Tues. |
| road | Rd. | mister | Mr. | avenue | Ave. |
| missus | Mrs. | October | Oct. | Friday | Fri. |
| before noon | A.M. | March | Mar. | August | Aug. |

**Directions:** Write each sentence using abbreviations.
1. On Monday at 9:00 before noon Mister Jones had a meeting.
On Mon. at 9:00 A.M., Mr. Jones had a meeting.
2. In December Doctor Carlson saw Missus Zuckerman.
In Dec., Dr. Carlson saw Mrs. Zuckerman.
3. One Tuesday in August Mister Wood went to the park.
One Tues. in Aug., Mr. Wood went to the park.

**34**

## Adjectives

**Adjectives** are words that tell more about nouns, such as a **happy** child, a **cold** day or a **hard** problem. Adjectives can tell how many (**one** airplane) or which one (**those** shoes).
**Directions:** The nouns are in bold letters. Circle the adjectives that describe the nouns.
**Example:** Some people have (unusual) **pets.**

1. Some people keep (wild) **animals,** like lions and bears.
2. (These) **pets** need special care.
3. (These) **animals** want to be free when they get older.
4. Even (small) **animals** can be difficult if they are wild.
5. Raccoons and squirrels are not (tame) **pets.**
6. Never touch a (wild) **animal** that may be sick.

Complete the story below by writing in your own adjectives. Use your imagination.

**My Cat**

My cat is a very _____ animal. She has

and _____ fur. Her _____ ball.

She has _____ _____ tail.

She has a _____ face and _____ whiskers.

I think she is the _____ cat in the world!

*Answers will vary.*

**35**

## Adjectives

**Directions:** Read the story below and underline the adjectives which are used in the story.

**The Best Soup I Ever Had**

I woke up <u>one</u> <u>cold</u> <u>winter</u> morning and decided to make a <u>delicious</u> pot of <u>hot</u> <u>vegetable</u> soup. The <u>first</u> vegetables I put in the <u>big</u> <u>grey</u> pot were <u>some</u> <u>sweet</u> <u>white</u> onions. Then I added <u>orange</u> carrots and <u>dark</u> <u>green</u> broccoli. The broccoli looked just like <u>little</u>, <u>tiny</u> trees. <u>Fresh</u>, <u>juicy</u> tomatoes and <u>crisp</u> potatoes were added next. I cooked it for a <u>long</u>, <u>long</u> time. <u>This</u> soup turned out to be the <u>best</u> soup I ever had.

Write two adjectives to describe each of the words below.

cucumber　long　peas _____
　　　　　green
spinach _____ _____

*Answers will vary.*

Now, rewrite two of the sentences from the story. Substitute your own adjectives for the words you underlined. Make your own soup.

_____
_____

*Answers will vary.*

**36**

## Adjectives and Nouns

**Directions:** Underline the noun in each sentence below. Then draw an arrow from each adjective to the noun it describes.
**Example:**
A platypus is a furry <u>animal</u> that lives in Australia.

1. This <u>animal</u> likes to swim.

2. The <u>nose</u> looks like a duck's <u>bill.</u>

3. It has a broad <u>tail</u> like a <u>beaver.</u>

4. <u>Platypuses</u> are great <u>swimmers.</u>

5. They have webbed <u>feet</u> which help them swim.

6. Their flat <u>tails</u> also help them move through the <u>water.</u>

7. The <u>platypus</u> is an unusual <u>mammal</u> because it lays eggs.

8. The <u>eggs</u> look like reptile <u>eggs.</u>

9. <u>Platypuses</u> can lay three <u>eggs</u> at a time.

10. These <u>babies</u> do not leave their <u>mothers</u> for one <u>year.</u>

11. This <u>animal</u> spends most of its <u>time</u> hunting near <u>streams.</u>

**37**

## Adjectives

A chart of adjectives can also be used to help describe nouns.

**Directions:** Look at the pictures. Complete each chart.

**Example:**

| Noun | What Color? | What Size? | What Number? |
|---|---|---|---|
| flower | red | small | two |

| Noun | What Color? | What Size? | What Number? |
|---|---|---|---|
| elephants | gray | large | two |

| Noun | What Color? | What Size? | What Number? |
|---|---|---|---|
| turtles | green | small | four |

| Noun | What Color? | What Size? | What Number? |
|---|---|---|---|
| tree | green | large | one |

**38**

**115**

## Prefixes

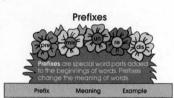

**Prefixes** are special word parts added to the beginnings of words. Prefixes change the meaning of words.

| Prefix | Meaning | Example |
|--------|---------|---------|
| un | not | **un**happy |
| re | again | **re**do |
| pre | before | **pre**view |
| mis | wrong | **mis**understanding |
| dis | opposite | **dis**obey |

**Directions:** Circle the word that begins with a prefix. Then write the prefix and the root word.

1. The dog was (unfriendly).  un + friendly
2. The movie (preview) was interesting.  pre + view
3. The referee called an (unfair) penalty.  un + fair
4. Please do not (misbehave).  mis + behave
5. My parents (disapprove) of that show.  dis + approve
6. I had to (redo) the assignment.  re + do

**39**

## Suffixes

**Suffixes** are word parts added to the ends of words. Suffixes change the meaning of words.

| Suffix | Meaning | Example |
|--------|---------|---------|
| able | able to be | lov**able** |
| less | without | sleep**less** |
| ful | full of | truth**ful** |
| y | having | snow**y** |

**Directions:** Circle the suffix in each word below.

**Example:** fluff(y)

rain(y)          thought(ful)          lik(able)

blame(less)      enjoy(able)          help(ful)

peace(ful)       care(less)           silk(y)

**Directions:** Write a word for each meaning.

full of hope _hopeful_          having rain _rainy_

without hope _hopeless_          able to break _breakable_

without power _powerless_          full of cheer _cheerful_

**40**

## Review

**Directions:** Circle the nouns that show ownership. Draw a box around the pronouns. Underline the adjectives. An example of each is done for you.

**Example:**
Tropical birds live in warm, wet lands.

1. They live in dark forests and busy zoos.
2. Their feathers are bright.
3. A canary is a small finch.
4. It is named for the Canary Islands.
5. Ben's birds are lovebirds.
6. He says they are small parrots that like to cuddle.
7. His parents gave him the lovebirds for his birthday.
8. Lisa's bird is a talking myna bird.
9. Her neighbors gave it to her when they moved.
10. She thanked them for the wonderful gift.
11. She says its feathers are dark with an orange mark on each wing.
12. Some children's myna birds can be very noisy.
13. Parakeets are this country's most popular tropical birds.
14. Parakeets' cages have ladders and swings.
15. A parakeet's diet is made up of seeds.

**41**

## Verbs

A **verb** is the action word in a sentence, the word that tells what something does or that something exists. **Examples: run, jump, skip.**

**Directions:** Draw a box around the verb in each sentence below.

1. Spiders spin webs of silk.
2. A spider waits in the center of the web for its meals.
3. A spider sinks its sharp fangs into insects.
4. Spiders eat many insects.
5. Spiders make their nests with silk.
6. Female spiders wrap silk around their eggs to protect them.

**Directions:** Choose the correct verb from the box and write it in the sentences below.

| hides | swims | eats | grabs | hurt |
|-------|-------|------|-------|------|

1. A crab spider _hides_ deep inside a flower where it cannot be seen.
2. The crab spider _grabs_ insects when they land on the flower.
3. The wolf spider is good because it _eats_ wasps.
4. The water spider _swims_ under water.
5. Most spiders will not _hurt_ people.

**42**

## Verbs

When a verb tells what one person or thing is doing now, it usually ends in **s. Example:** She sings.
When a verb is used with **you, I** or **we,** we do not add an **s.**
**Example:** I sing.

**Directions:** Write the correct verb in each sentence.

**Example:**
I _write_ a newspaper about our street.  **writes, write**

1. My sister _helps_ me sometimes.  **helps, help**
2. She _draws_ the pictures.  **draw, draws**
3. We _deliver_ them together.  **delivers, deliver**
4. I _tell_ the news about all the people.  **tell, tells**
5. Mr. Macon _grows_ the most beautiful flowers.  **grow, grows**
6. Mrs. Jones _talks_ to her plants.  **talks, talk**
7. Kevin Turner _lets_ his dog loose everyday.  **lets, let**
8. Little Mikey Smith _gets_ lost once a week.  **get, gets**
9. You may _think_ I live on an interesting street.  **thinks, think**
10. We _say_ it's the best street in town.  **say, says**

**43**

## Helping Verbs

A **helping verb** is a word used with an action verb.

**Examples: might, shall** and **are**

**Directions:** Write a helping verb from the box with each action verb.

| can | could | must | might |
|-----|-------|------|-------|
| may | would | should | will |
| shall | did | does | do |
| had | have | has | am |
| are | were | is | |
| be | being | been | |

**Example: Answers will vary but may include:**
Tomorrow, I _might_ play soccer.

1. Mom _may_ buy my new soccer shoes tonight.
2. Yesterday, my old soccer shoes _were_ ripped by the cat.
3. I _am_ going to ask my brother to go to the game.
4. He usually _does_ not like soccer.
5. But, he _will_ go with me because I am his sister.
6. He _has_ promised to watch the entire soccer game.
7. He has _been_ helping me with my homework.
8. I _can_ spell a lot better because of his help.
9. Maybe I _could_ finish the semester at the top of my class.

**44**

## Past-Tense Verbs

The **past tense** of a verb tells about something that has already happened. We add a **d** or an **ed** to most verbs to show that something has already happened.

**Directions:** Use the verb from the first sentence to complete the second sentence.

**Example:**

Please **walk** the dog.   I already _walked_ her.

1. The flowers look good.   They _looked_ better yesterday.
2. Please accept my gift.   I _accepted_ it for my sister.
3. I wonder who will win.   I _wondered_ about it all night.
4. He will saw the wood.   He _sawed_ some last week.
5. Fold the paper neatly.   She _folded_ her paper.
6. Let's cook outside tonight.   We _cooked_ outside last night.
7. Do not block the way.   They _blocked_ the entire street.
8. Form the clay this way.   He _formed_ it into a ball.
9. Follow my car.   We _followed_ them down the street.
10. Glue the pages like this.   She _glued_ the flowers on.

**45**

## Present-Tense Verbs

The **present tense** of a verb tells about something that is happening now, happens often or is about to happen. These verbs can be written two ways: The bird sing**s**. The bird **is** sing**ing**.

**Directions:** Write each sentence again, using the verb **is** and writing the **ing** form of the verb.

**Example:**   He cooks the cheeseburgers.
_He is cooking the cheeseburgers._

1. Sharon dances to that song.
_Sharon is dancing to that song._
2. Frank washed the car.
_Frank is washing the car._
3. Mr. Benson smiles at me.
_Mr. Benson is smiling at me._

Write a verb for the sentences below that tells something that is happening now. Be sure to use the verb **is** and the **ing** form of the verb.

**Example:** The big, brown dog _is barking_ .

1. The little baby _____ .
2. Most nine-year-olds _____
3. The monster on television _____

_Answers will vary._

**46**

## Future-Tense Verbs

The **future tense** of a verb tells about something that has not happened yet but will happen in the future. **Will** or **shall** are usually used with future tense.

**Directions:** Change the verb tense in each sentence to future tense.

**Example:** She cooks dinner.
_She will cook dinner._

1. He plays baseball.
_He will play baseball._
2. She walks to school.
_She will walk to school._
3. Bobby talks to the teacher.
_Bobby will talk to the teacher._
4. I remember to vote.
_I will remember to vote._
5. Jack mows the lawn every week.
_Jack will mow the lawn every week._
6. We go on vacation soon.
_We will go on vacation soon._

**47**

## Review

**Verb tenses** can be in the past, present or future.

**Directions:** Match each sentence with the correct verb tense. **(Think:** When did each thing happen?)

It will rain tomorrow. — past
He played golf. — present
Molly is sleeping. — future
Jack is singing a song. — past
I shall buy a kite. — present
Dad worked hard today. — future

*Past*
*Present*
*Future*

**Directions:** Change the verb to the tense shown.

1. Jenny played with her new friend. (present)
_Jenny is playing with her new friend._
2. Bobby is talking to him. (future)
_Bobby will talk to him._
3. Holly and Angie walk here. (past)
_Holly and Angie walked here._

**48**

## Irregular Verbs

**Irregular verbs** are verbs that do not change from the present tense to the past tense in the regular way with **d** or **ed**.
**Example:** sing, sang
**Directions:** Read the sentence and underline the verbs. Choose the past-tense form from the box and write it next to the sentence.

| | |
|---|---|
| blow — blew | fly — flew |
| come — came | give — gave |
| take — took | wear — wore |
| make — made | sing — sang |
| grow — grew | |

**Example:**
Dad will _make_ a cake tonight.   _made_

1. I will probably _grow_ another inch this year.   _grew_
2. I will _blow_ out the candles.   _blew_
3. Everyone will _give_ me presents.   _gave_
4. I will _wear_ my favorite red shirt.   _wore_
5. My cousins will _come_ from out of town.   _came_
6. It will _take_ them four hours.   _took_
7. My Aunt Betty will _fly_ in from Cleveland.   _flew_
8. She will _sing_ me a song when she gets here.   _sang_

**49**

## Irregular Verbs

**Directions:** Circle the verb that completes each sentence.

1. Scientists will try to (find, found) the cure.
2. Eric (brings, brought) his lunch to school yesterday.
3. Everyday, Betsy (sings, sang) all the way home.
4. Jason (breaks, broke) the vase last night.
5. The ice had (freezes, frozen) in the tray.
6. Mitzi has (swims, swum) in that pool before.
7. Now I (choose, chose) to exercise daily.
8. The teacher has (rings, rung) the bell.
9. The boss (speaks, spoke) to us yesterday.
10. She (says, said) it twice already.

**50**

## Irregular Verbs

The verb **be** is different from all other verbs. The present-tense forms of **be** are **am**, **is** and **are**. The past-tense forms of **be** are **was** and **were**. The verb **to be** is written in the following ways:

**singular:** I am, you are, he is, she is, it is
**plural:** we are, you are, they are

**Directions:** Choose the correct form of **be** from the words in the box and write it in each sentence.

| are | am | is | was | were |
|---|---|---|---|---|

**Example:**  Answers will vary, but may include:
I ___am___ feeling good at this moment.

1. My sister ___is___ a good singer.
2. You ___are___ going to the store with me.
3. Sandy ___was___ at the movies last week.
4. Rick and Tom ___are___ best friends.
5. He ___is___ happy about the surprise.
6. The cat ___is___ hungry.
7. I ___am___ going to the ball game.
8. They ___are___ silly.
9. I ___am___ glad to help my mother.

**51**

## Linking Verbs

**Linking verbs** connect the noun to a descriptive word. Linking verbs are often forms of the verb **be**.

**Directions:** The linking verb is underlined in each sentence. Circle the two words that are being connected.

**Example:** The (cat) is (fat.)

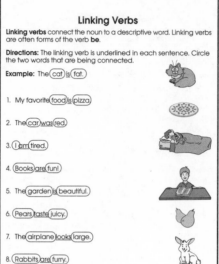

1. My favorite (food) is (pizza.)
2. The (car) was (red.)
3. (I) am (tired.)
4. (Books) are (fun!)
5. The (garden) is (beautiful.)
6. (Pears) taste (juicy.)
7. The (airplane) looks (large.)
8. (Rabbits) are (furry.)

**52**

## Review

**Directions:** Write the correct verb in each sentence below.

1. Before the wheel, people ___dragged___ heavy loads.   drag, dragged
2. No one knows who ___invented___ the wheel.   invented, invent
3. The Sumerians ___were___ some of the first people to use the wheel.   were, are
4. They ___made___ the first wheels of wood and stone.   make, made
5. The wheels ___were___ very heavy.   be, were
6. Then people ___thought___ of spokes.   think, thought
7. Spokes helped the wheels ___turn___ more easily.   turn, turned
8. Soon, people were ___building___ roads.   built, building
9. I ___am___ glad that the wheel was invented.   is, am
10. We ___have___ many things with wheels.   has, have
11. Cars and trucks ___have___ wheels.   has, have
12. Potters ___made___ pots on a wheel.   make, made
13. Wool is ___spun___ on a spinning wheel.   spin, spun
14. Amusement park rides ___have___ wheels.   have, has
15. My favorite set of wheels ___is___ on my bike.   is, am

**53**

## Adverbs

**Adverbs** are words that describe verbs. They tell where, how or when.

**Directions:** Circle the adverb in each of the following sentences.

**Example:** The doctor worked (carefully.)

1. The skater moved (gracefully) across the ice.
2. Their call was returned (quickly.)
3. We (easily) learned the new words.
4. He did the work (perfectly.)
5. She lost her purse (somewhere.)

Complete the sentences below by writing your own adverbs in the blanks.

**Example:** The bees worked ___busily___.

1. The dog barked _____
2. The baby smiled _____
3. She wrote her name _____
4. The horse ran _____

Answers may vary.

**54**

## Adverbs

**Directions:** Read each sentence. Then answer the questions on the lines below.

**Example:** Charles ate hungrily.
who? ___Charles___
what? ___ate___
how? ___hungrily___

1. She dances slowly.
who? ___She___
what? ___dances___
how? ___slowly___

2. The girl spoke carefully.
who? ___girl___
what? ___spoke___
how? ___carefully___

3. My brother ran quickly.
who? ___brother___
what? ___ran___
how? ___quickly___

4. Jean walks home often.
who? ___Jean___
what? ___walks___
when? ___often___

5. The children played there.
who? ___children___
what? ___played___
where? ___there___

**55**

## Prepositions

**Prepositions** show relationships between the noun or pronoun and another noun in the sentence. The preposition comes before that noun.

**Example:** The <u>book</u> is (on) the <u>table</u>.

| Common Prepositions | | | | |
|---|---|---|---|---|
| above | behind | by | near | over |
| across | below | in | off | through |
| around | beside | inside | on | under |

**Directions:** Circle the prepositions in each sentence.

1. The dog ran fast (around) the house.
2. The plates (in) the cupboard were clean.
3. Put the card (inside) the envelope.
4. The towel (on) the sink was wet.
5. I planted flowers (in) my garden.
6. My kite flew high (above) the trees.
7. The chair (near) the counter was sticky.
8. (Under) the ground, worms lived (in) their homes.
9. I put the bow (around) the box.
10. (Beside) the pond, there was a playground.

**56**

### Articles

**Articles** are words used before nouns. **A**, **an** and **the** are articles. We use **a** before words that begin with a consonant. We use **an** before words that begin with a vowel.

**Example:**   a peach    an apple

**Directions:** Write **a** or **an** in the sentences below.

**Example:** My bike had ___a___ flat tire.

1. They brought ___a___ goat to the farm.
2. My mom wears ___an___ old pair of shoes to mow the lawn.
3. We had ___a___ party for my grandfather.
4. Everybody had ___an___ ice-cream cone after the game.
5. We bought ___a___ picnic table for our backyard.
6. We saw ___a___ lion sleeping in the shade.
7. It was ___an___ evening to be remembered.
8. He brought ___a___ blanket to the game.
9. ___An___ exit sign was above the door.
10. They went to ___an___ orchard to pick apples.
11. He ate ___an___ orange for lunch.

**57**

---

### Commas

**Commas** are used to separate words in a series of three or more.
**Example:** My favorite fruits are apples, bananas and oranges.

**Directions:** Put commas where they are needed in each sentence.

1. Please buy milk, eggs, bread and cheese.

2. I need a folder, paper and pencils for school.

3. Some good pets are cats, dogs, gerbils, fish and rabbits.

4. Aaron, Mike and Matt went to the baseball game.

5. Major forms of transportation are planes, trains and automobiles.

**58**

---

### Articles and Commas

**Directions:** Write **a** or **an** in each blank. Put commas where they are needed in the paragraphs below.

**Owls**

___An___ owl is ___a___ bird of prey. This means it hunts small animals. Owls catch insects, fish and birds. Mice are ___an___ owl's favorite dinner. Owls like protected places, such as trees, burrows or barns. Owls make noises that sound like hoots, screeches or even barks. ___An___ owl's feathers may be black, brown, gray or white.

**A Zoo for You**

___A___ zoo is ___an___ excellent place for keeping animals. Zoos have mammals, birds, reptiles and amphibians. Some zoos have domestic animals, such as rabbits, sheep and goats. Another name for this type of zoo is ___a___ petting zoo. In some zoos, elephants, lions and tigers live in open country. This is because ___an___ enormous animal needs open space for roaming.

**59**

---

### Commas

We use commas to separate the day from the year.
**Example:** May 13, 1950

**Directions:** Write the dates in the blanks. Put the commas in and capitalize the name of each month.

**Example:**
Jack and Dave were born on february 22 1982.
___February 22, 1982___
1. My father's birthday is may 19 1948.
___May 19, 1948___
2. My sister was fourteen on december 13 1994.
___December 13, 1994___
3. Lauren's seventh birthday was on november 30 1998.
___November 30, 1998___
4. october 13 1996 was the last day I saw my lost cat.
___October 13, 1996___
5. On april 17 1997, we saw the Grand Canyon.
___April 17, 1997___
6. Our vacation lasted from april 2 1998 to april 26 1998.
___April 2, 1998___   ___April 26, 1998___
7. Molly's baby sister was born on august 14 1991.
___August 14, 1991___
8. My mother was born on june 22 1959.
___June 22, 1959___

**60**

---

### Capitalization

The names of **people**, **places** and **pets**, the **days of the week**, the **months of the year** and **holidays** begin with a capital letter.
**Directions:** Read the words in the box. Write the words in the correct column with capital letters at the beginning of each word.

| | | | |
|---|---|---|---|
| ron polsky | tuesday | march | april |
| presidents' day | saturday | woofy | october |
| blackie | portland, oregon | corning, new york | molly yoder |
| valentine's day | fluffy | harold edwards | arbor day |
| bozeman, montana | sunday | | |

| **People** | **Places** | **Pets** |
|---|---|---|
| Ron Polsky | Bozeman, Montana | Blackie |
| Harold Edwards | Portland, Oregon | Fluffy |
| Molly Yoder | Corning, New York | Woofy |

| **Days** | **Months** | **Holidays** |
|---|---|---|
| Tuesday | March | Valentine's Day |
| Saturday | April | Presidents' Day |
| Sunday | October | Arbor Day |

**61**

---

### Commas

We capitalize the names of cities and states. We use a comma to separate the name of a city and a state.

**Directions:** Use capital letters and commas to write the names of the cities and states correctly.

**Example:**
sioux falls south dakota   ___Sioux Falls, South Dakota___

1. plymouth massachusetts   ___Plymouth, Massachusetts___
2. boston massachusetts   ___Boston, Massachusetts___
3. philadelphia pennsylvania   ___Philadelphia, Pennsylvania___
4. white plains new york   ___White Plains, New York___
5. newport rhode island   ___Newport, Rhode Island___
6. yorktown virginia   ___Yorktown, Virginia___
7. nashville tennessee   ___Nashville, Tennessee___
8. portland oregon   ___Portland, Oregon___
9. mansfield ohio   ___Mansfield, Ohio___

**62**

## Review

**Directions:** Write an adverb from the box in the sentences below to tell how, when or where something happens.

| merrily | carefully | thoroughly | there | always | sometimes |

1. The coach always makes us stretch our muscles _carefully_ (how?).

2. Katie is _always_ (when?) the perfect guest when she visits.

3. The canaries sang _merrily_ (how?) in their cages.

4. He hit the ball way over _there_ (where?).

**Directions:** Read the words in the box. Circle the word if **an** should be used as the article before the word. Underline the word if **a** should be used as the article before the word.

| bath | cake | (owl) | (apple) | (ice) | cookie |
| beach | umbrella | (onion) | (oven) | dress | shoe |
| girl | boy | (egg) | elf | foot | book |

**Directions:** Use commas and capital letters to write the following dates and places correctly.

1. february 6 1996 — _February 6, 1996_
2. johnson wisconsin — _Johnson, Wisconsin_
3. september 20 1998 — _September 20, 1998_
4. cheyenne wyoming — _Cheyenne, Wyoming_

**63**

## Parts of Speech

Nouns, pronouns, verbs, adjectives, adverbs and prepositions are all **parts of speech**.

**Directions:** Label the words in each sentence with the correct part of speech.

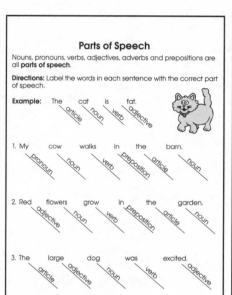

Example: The _article_ cat _noun_ is _verb_ fat. _adjective_

1. My _pronoun_ cow _noun_ walks _verb_ in _preposition_ the _article_ barn. _noun_

2. Red _adjective_ flowers _noun_ grow _verb_ in _preposition_ the _article_ garden. _noun_

3. The _article_ large _adjective_ dog _noun_ was _verb_ excited. _adjective_

**64**

## Parts of Speech

**Directions:** Ask someone to give you nouns, verbs, adjectives and pronouns where shown. Write them in the blanks. Read the story to your friend when you finish.

The _____ (adjective) Adventure

I went for a _____ (noun). I found a really big _____ (noun).

It was so _____ (adjective) that I _____ (verb) all the

way home. I put it in my _____ (noun) my amazement, it

began to _____ (verb) took it to my

_____ (place). I she **Answers will vary.** _____ (plural noun).

I decided _____ it in a box and wrap it up with

_____ (adjective) paper. I gave it to _____ (person) for a

present. When _____ (pronoun) opened it, _____ (pronoun)

_____ (past-tense verb) _____ (pronoun) shouted, "Thank you!

This is the best _____ (noun) I've ever had!"

**65**

## Parts of Speech

**Directions:** Write the part of speech of each underlined word.

NOUN PRONOUN VERB ADJECTIVE ADVERB PREPOSITION

① ②
There <u>are</u> many <u>different</u> kinds of animals. Some animals live in the
③
wild. Some animals live in the <u>zoo</u>. And still others live in homes. The animals
④
that <u>live</u> in homes are called pets.

There are many types of pets. Some pets without fur are fish, turtles,
⑤ ⑥
snakes and hermit crabs. Trained birds can fly <u>around</u> <u>your</u> house. Some
⑦
<u>furry</u> animals are cats, dogs, rabbits, ferrets, gerbils or hamsters. Some animals
⑧ ⑨
can <u>successfully</u> learn tricks that <u>you</u> teach them. Whatever your favorite
⑩
animal is, animals can be <u>special</u> friends!

1. _verb_    4. _verb_

2. _adjective_   5. _preposition_   7. _adjective_   9. _pronoun_

3. _noun_    6. _pronoun_   8. _adverb_   10. _adjective_

**66**

## And and But

We can use **and** or **but** to make one longer sentence from two short ones.

**Directions:** Use **and** or **but** to make two short sentences into a longer, more interesting one. Write the new sentence on the line below the two short sentences.

**Example:**
The skunk has black fur. The skunk has a white stripe.

_The skunk has black fur and a white stripe._

1. The skunk has a small head. The skunk has small ears.

_The skunk has a small head and small ears._

2. The skunk has short legs. Skunks can move quickly.

_The skunk has short legs but can move easily._

3. Skunks sleep in hollow trees. Skunk sleep underground.

_Skunks sleep in hollow trees and underground._

4. Skunks are chased by animals. Skunks do not run away.

_Skunks are chased by animals but do not run away._

5. Skunks sleep during the day. Skunks hunt at night.

_Skunks sleep during the day and hunt at night._

**67**

## Subjects

A **subject** tells who or what the sentence is about.

**Directions:** Underline the subject in the following sentences.

**Example:**
<u>The zebra</u> is a large animal.

1. <u>Zebras</u> live in Africa.

2. <u>Zebras</u> are related to horses.

3. <u>Horses</u> have longer hair than zebras.

4. <u>Zebras</u> are good runners.

5. <u>Their feet</u> are protected by their hooves.

6. <u>Some animals</u> live in groups.

7. <u>These groups</u> are called herds.

8. <u>Zebras</u> live in herds with other grazing animals.

9. <u>Grazing animals</u> eat mostly grass.

10. <u>They</u> usually eat three times a day.

11. <u>They</u> often travel to water holes.

**68**

## Predicates

A **predicate** tells what the subject is doing, has done or will do.

**Directions:** Underline the predicate in the following sentences.

**Example:** Woodpeckers live in trees.

1. They hunt for insects in the trees.

2. Woodpeckers have strong beaks.

3. They can peck through the bark.

4. The pecking sound can be heard from far away.

**Directions:** Circle the groups of words that can be predicates.

(have long tongues)          (pick up insects)

hole in bark                      sticky substance

(help it to climb trees)        tree bark

Now, choose the correct predicates from above to finish these sentences.

1. Woodpeckers          have long tongues

2. They use their tongues to          pick up insects

3. Its strong feet          help it to climb trees .

69

---

## Subjects and Predicates

**Directions:** Write the words for the subject to answer the **who** or **what** questions. Write the words for the predicate to answer the **does**, **did**, **is** or **has** questions.

**Example:**

My friend has two pairs of sunglasses.  who? _My friend_
has? _has two pairs of sunglasses._

1. John's dog went to school with him.  what? _John's dog_
did? _went to school with him._

2. The Eskimo traveled by dog sled.  who? _The Eskimo_
did? _traveled by dog sled._

3. Alex slept in his treehouse last night.  who? _Alex_
did? _slept in his treehouse last night_

4. Cherry pie is my favorite kind of pie.  what? _Cherry pie_
is? _is my favorite kind of pie._

5. The mail carrier brings the mail to the door.  who? _The mail carrier_
does? _brings the mail to the door._

6. We have more than enough bricks to build the wall.  who? _We_
has? _have more than enough bricks to build the wall._

7. The bird has a worm in its beak.  what? _The bird_
has? _has a worm in its beak._

70

---

## Subjects and Predicates

**Directions:** Every sentence has two main parts—the subject and the predicate. Draw one line under the subject and two lines under the predicate in each sentence below.

**Example:**

Porcupines are related to mice and rats.

1. They are large rodents.

2. Porcupines have long, sharp quills.

3. The quills stand up straight when it is angry.

4. Most animals stay away from porcupines.

5. Their quills hurt other animals.

6. Porcupines sleep under rocks or bushes.

7. They sleep during the day.

8. Porcupines eat plants at night.

9. North America has some porcupines.

10. They are called New World porcupines.

11. New World porcupines can climb trees.

71

---

## Subjects and Predicates

**Directions:** Draw one line under the subjects and two lines under the predicates in the sentences below.

1. My mom likes to plant flowers.

2. Our neighbors walk their dog.

3. Our car needs gas.

4. The children play house.

5. Movies and popcorn go well together.

6. Peanut butter and jelly is my favorite kind of sandwich.

7. Bill, Sue and Nancy ride to the park.

8. We use pencils, markers and pens to write on paper.

9. Trees and shrubs need special care.

72

---

## Simple Subjects

A **simple subject** is the main noun or pronoun in the complete subject.

**Directions:** Draw a line between the subject and the predicate. Circle the simple subject.

**Example:** The black (bear) lives in the zoo.

1. (Penguins) look like they wear tuxedos.

2. The (seal) enjoys raw fish.

3. The (monkeys) like to swing on bars.

4. The beautiful (peacock) has colorful feathers.

5. (Bats) like dark places.

6. Some (snakes) eat small rodents.

7. The orange and brown (giraffes) have long necks.

8. The baby (zebra) is close to his mother.

73

---

## Compound Subjects

**Compound subjects** are two or more nouns that have the same predicate.

**Directions:** Combine the subjects to create one sentence with a compound subject.

**Example:** Jill can swing.
Whitney can swing.
Luke can swing.
Jill, Whitney and Luke can swing.

1. Roses grow in the garden. Tulips grow in the garden.

Roses and tulips grow in the garden.

2. Apples are fruit. Oranges are fruit. Bananas are fruit.

Apples, oranges and bananas are fruit.

3. Bears live in the zoo. Monkeys live in the zoo.

Bears and monkeys live in the zoo.

4. Jackets keep us warm. Sweaters keep us warm.

Jackets and sweaters keep us warm.

74

## Compound Subjects

**Directions:** Underline the simple subjects in each compound subject.

**Example:** <u>Dogs</u> and <u>cats</u> are good pets.

1. <u>Blueberries</u> and <u>strawberries</u> are fruit.

2. <u>Jesse</u>, <u>Jake</u> and <u>Hannah</u> like school.

3. <u>Cows</u>, <u>pigs</u> and <u>sheep</u> live on a farm.

4. <u>Boys</u> and <u>girls</u> ride the bus.

5. <u>My family</u> and <u>I</u> took a trip to Duluth.

6. <u>Fruits</u> and <u>vegetables</u> are good for you.

7. <u>Katarina</u>, <u>Lexi</u> and <u>Mandi</u> like to go swimming.

8. <u>Petunias</u>, <u>impatiens</u>, <u>snapdragons</u> and <u>geraniums</u> are all flowers.

9. <u>Coffee</u>, <u>tea</u> and <u>milk</u> are beverages.

10. <u>Dave</u>, <u>Karla</u> and <u>Tami</u> worked on the project together.

**75**

## Simple Predicates

A **simple predicate** is the main verb or verbs in the complete predicate.

**Directions:** Draw a line between the complete subject and the complete predicate. Circle the simple predicate.

**Example:** The ripe apples | (fell) to the ground.

1. The farmer | (scattered) feed for the chickens.

2. The horses | (galloped) wildly around the corral.

3. The baby chicks | were (staying) warm by the light.

4. The tractor | was (bailing) hay.

5. The silo | (was) full of grain.

6. The cows | were (being) milked.

7. The milk truck | (drove) up to the barn.

8. The rooster | (woke) everyone up.

**76**

## Compound Predicates

**Compound predicates** have two or more verbs that have the same subject.

**Directions:** Combine the predicates to create one sentence with a compound predicate.

**Example:** We went to the zoo.
We watched the monkeys.
We went to the zoo and watched the monkeys.

1. Students read their books. Students do their work.

Students read their books and do their work.

2. Dogs can bark loudly. Dogs can do tricks.

Dogs can bark loudly and do tricks.

3. The football player caught the ball. The football player ran.

The football player caught the ball and ran.

4. My dad sawed wood. My dad stacked wood.

My dad sawed and stacked wood.

5. My teddy bear is soft. My teddy bear likes to be hugged.

My teddy bear is soft and likes to be hugged.

**77**

## Compound Predicates

**Directions:** Underline the simple predicates (verbs) in each predicate.

**Example:** The fans <u>clapped</u> and <u>cheered</u> at the game.

1. The coach <u>talks</u> and <u>encourages</u> the team.

2. The cheerleaders <u>jump</u> and <u>yell</u>.

3. The basketball players <u>dribble</u> and <u>shoot</u> the ball.

4. The basketball <u>bounces</u> and <u>hits</u> the backboard.

5. The ball <u>rolls</u> around the rim and <u>goes</u> into the basket.

6. Everyone <u>leaps</u> up and <u>cheers</u>.

7. The team <u>scores</u> and <u>wins</u>!

**78**

## Subjects

**Directions:** Use your own words to write the subjects in the sentences below.

1. _____ landed in my backyard.
2. _____ rushed out of the house.
3. _____ had bright lights.
4. _____ were tall and green.
5. _____ talked to me.
6. _____ came outside with me.
7. _____ ran into the house.
8. _____ shook hands.
9. _____ said funny things.
10. _____ gave us a ride.
11. _____ flew away.
12. _____ will come back soon.

*Answers will vary.*

**79**

## Predicates

**Directions:** Use your own words to write the predicates in the sentences below.

1. The swimming pool _____
2. The water _____
3. The sun _____
4. I always _____
5. My friends _____
6. We always _____
7. The lifeguard _____
8. The rest periods _____
9. The lunch _____
10. My favorite food _____
11. The diving board _____
12. We never _____

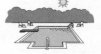
*Answers will vary.*

**80**

## Review

**Directions:** Use **and** or **but** to make longer, more interesting sentences from two shorter sentences.

1. I have a dog. I have a cat.

I have a dog and a cat.

2. The sun is shining. The weather is cold.

The sun is shining, but the weather is cold.

**Directions:** Draw one line under the subjects in the sentences. Draw two lines under the predicates.

1. We went on a white water rafting trip.

2. Sam and Ben won the best prize.

3. She painted a picture for me.

4. Those flowers are beautiful.

5. She is a great babysitter.

6. My shoes got wet in the creek.

7. The cows are not in the barn.

8. He has a new shirt for the party.

**81**

## Word Order

**Word order** is the logical order of words in sentences.

**Directions:** Put the words in order so that each sentence tells a complete idea.

**Example:** outside put cat the

Put the cat outside.

1. mouse the ate snake the

The snake ate the mouse.

2. dog John his walk took a for

John took his dog for a walk.

3. birthday Maria the present wrapped

Maria wrapped the birthday present.

4. escaped parrot the cage its from

The parrot escaped from its cage.

5. to soup quarts water three of add the

Add three quarts of water to the soup.

6. bird the bushes into the chased cat the

The cat chased the bird into the bushes.

**82**

## Sentences and Non-Sentences

A **sentence** tells a complete idea.

**Directions:** Circle the groups of words that tell a complete idea.

1. (Sharks are fierce hunters.)

2. Afraid of sharks.

3. (The great white shark will attack people.)

4. (Other kinds will not.)

5. (Sharks have an outer row of teeth for grabbing food.)

6. (When the outer teeth fall out, another row of teeth moves up.)

7. Keep the ocean clean by eating dead animals.

8. Not a single bone in its body.

9. Cartilage.

10. Made of the same material as the tip of your nose.

11. (Unlike other fish, sharks cannot float.)

12. In motion constantly.

13. Even while sleeping.

**83**

## Completing a Story

**Directions:** Complete the story, using sentences that tell complete ideas.

One morning, my friend asked me to take my first bus trip downtown. I was so excited I _____

_____

At the bus stop, we saw_____. Our bus driver

_____

When we got off the bus _____

*Answers will vary.*

_____. I'd never seen so many

My favorite part was when we _____

We stopped to eat _____

_____. I bought a _____

_____.

When we got home, I told my friend, "_____

_____."

**84**

## Complete the Sentences

**Directions:** Write your own endings to make the sentences tell a complete idea.

**Example:**

*The Wizard of Oz* is a story about <u>Dorothy and her dog, Toto</u>.

1. Dorothy and Toto live on _____

2. A big storm _____

3. Dorothy and Toto are carried off to _____

4. Dorothy meets _____

5. Dorothy, Toto and their friends follow the _____

6. Dorothy tries to find _____

7. The Wizard turns out to be _____

8. A scary person in the story is _____

*Answers will vary.*

9. The wicked witch is killed by _____

10. The hot air balloon leaves without _____

11. Dorothy uses her magic shoes to _____

**85**

## Complete the Sentences

**Directions:** Write your own endings to make the sentences tell a complete idea.

**Example:**

*Cinderella* is a story about <u>Cinderella, her stepmother, stepsisters and the prince.</u>

1. Cinderella lives with. _____

2. Her stepmother and her stepsisters _____

3. Cinderella's stepsisters receive _____

4. Cinderella cannot go to the ball because _____

_____

5. The fairy godmother comes _____

6. The prince dances with *Answers will vary.*

7. When the clock strikes midnight, _____

8. The prince's men look for _____

9. The slipper fits _____

10. Cinderella and the prince live _____

**86**

## Alliteration

**Alliteration** is the repeated use of beginning sounds. Alliterative sentences are sometimes referred to as tongue twisters.

**Example:**

She sells sea shells by the seashore.
Peter Piper picked a peck of pickled peppers.

**Directions:** Use alliteration to write your own tongue twisters.

1. _____

_____

2. _____

*Answers will vary.*

3. _____

_____

---

## Statements and Questions

**Statements** are sentences that tell about something. Statements begin with a capital letter and end with a period. **Questions** are sentences that ask about something. Questions begin with a capital letter and end with a question mark.

**Directions:** Rewrite the sentences using capital letters and either a period or a question mark.

**Example:** walruses live in the Arctic

Walruses live in the Arctic.

1. are walruses large sea mammals or fish

Are walruses large sea mammals or fish?

2. they spend most of their time in the water and on ice

They spend most of their time in the water and on ice.

3. are floating sheets of ice called ice floes

Are floating sheets of ice called ice floes?

4. are walruses related to seals

Are walruses related to seals?

5. their skin is thick, wrinkled and almost hairless

Their skin is thick, wrinkled and almost hairless.

---

## Statements and Questions

**Directions:** Change the statements into questions and the questions into statements.

**Example:** Jane is happy.      Is Jane happy?
Were you late?      You were late.

1. The rainbow was brightly colored.

Is the rainbow brightly colored?

2. Was the sun coming out?

The sun was coming out.

3. The dog is doing tricks.

Is the dog doing tricks?

4. Have you washed the dishes today?

You have washed the dishes today.

5. Kurt was the circus ringmaster.

Was Kurt the circus ringmaster?

6. Were you planning on going to the library?

You were planning on going to the library.

---

87

88

89

---

## Exclamations

**Exclamation points** are used for sentences that express strong feelings. These sentences can have one or two words or be very long.

**Example: Wait!** or **Don't forget to call!**

**Directions:** Add an exclamation point at the end of sentences that express strong feelings. Add a period at the end of the statements.

1. My parents and I were watching television.
2. The snow began falling around noon.
3. Wow!
4. The snow was really coming down!
5. We turned the television off and looked out the window.
6. The snow looked like a white blanket.
7. How beautiful!
8. We decided to put on our coats and go outside.
9. Hurry!
10. Get your sled.
11. All the people on the street came out to see the snow.
12. How wonderful!
13. The children began making a snowman.
14. What a great day!

---

## Review

There are three kinds of sentences.

**Statements:** Sentences that tell something. Statements end with a period (.).
**Questions:** Sentences that ask a question. Questions end with a question mark (?).
**Exclamations:** Sentences that express a strong feeling. Exclamations end with an exclamation point (!).

**Directions:** Write what kind of sentence each is.

1. Exclamation    What a super day to go to the zoo!
2. Question    Do you like radishes?
3. Statement    I belong to the chess club.
4. Statement    Wash the dishes.
5. Question    How much does that cost?
6. Statement    Apples grow on trees.
7. Statement    Look out the window.
8. Exclamation    Look at the colorful rainbow!

---

## Contractions

**Contractions** are shortened forms of two words. We use apostrophes to show where letters are missing.

**Example: It is = it's**

**Directions:** Write the words that are used in each contraction.

we're   we + are        they'll   they + will
you'll   you + will      aren't   are + not
I'm    I + am          isn't   is + not

**Directions:** Write the contraction for the two words shown.

you have   you've        have not   haven't
had not   hadn't        we will   we'll
they are   they're       he is   he's
she had   she'd        it will   it'll
I am    I'm          is not   isn't

---

90

91

92

## Apostrophes

**Apostrophes** are used to show ownership by placing an **s** at the end of a single person, place or thing.

**Example:** Mary's cat

**Directions:** Write the apostrophes in the contractions below.

**Example:** We shouldn't be going to their house so late at night.

1. We didn't think that the ice cream would melt so fast.

2. They're never around when we're ready to go.

3. Didn't you need to make a phone call?

4. Who's going to help you paint the bicycle red?

**Directions:** Add an apostrophe and an **s** to the words to show ownership of a person, place or thing.

**Example:** Jill's bike is broken.

1. That is Holly's flower garden.

2. Mark's new skates are black and green.

3. Mom threw away Dad's old shoes.

4. Buster's food dish was lost in the snowstorm.

93

## Quotation Marks

**Quotation marks** are punctuation marks that tell what is said by a person. Quotation marks go before the first word and after the punctuation of a direct quote. The first word of a direct quote begins with a capital letter.

**Example:** Katie said, "Never go in the water without a friend."

**Directions:** Put quotation marks around the correct words in the sentences below.

**Example:** "Wait for me, please," said Laura.

1. "John, would you like to visit a jungle?" asked his uncle.

2. The police officer said, "Don't worry, we'll help you."

3. James shouted, "Hit a home run!"

4. My friend Carol said, "I really don't like cheeseburgers."

**Directions:** Write your own quotations by answering the questions below. Be sure to put quotation marks around your words.

1. What would you say if you saw a di_____

_____

*Answers will vary.*

2. What would your _____ if your hair turned purple?

_____

94

## Quotation Marks

**Directions:** Put quotation marks around the correct words in the sentences below.

1. Can we go for a bike ride? asked Katrina.

"Can we go for a bike ride?" asked Katrina.

2. Yes, said Mom.

"Yes," said Mom.

3. Let's go to the park, said Mike.

"Let's go to the park," said Mike.

4. Great idea! said Mom.

"Great idea!" said Mom.

5. How long until we get there? asked Katrina.

"How long until we get there?" asked Katrina.

6. Soon, said Mike.

"Soon," said Mike.

7. Here we are! exclaimed Mom.

"Here we are!" exclaimed Mom.

95

## Review

**Directions:** Unscramble this sentence and write it on the line below.

1. have tails short bodies wide and pigs

Pigs have wide bodies and short tails.

**Directions:** Put a question mark, a period or an exclamation point at the end of the following sentences:

1. Tiny pigs, called miniature pigs, weigh only 60 pounds.

2. Pigs can weigh as much as 800 pounds.

3. Wow!

4. Do pigs have spots?

**Directions:** Put the apostrophes in the sentences to replace a letter or to show ownership.

1. A pig's pen should have water in it.

2. They're really not animals that like mud.

3. It's an animal that needs water to keep cool.

4. Most farmers don't give them their own pools.

**Directions:** Put quotation marks in the sentences below.

1. "You eat like a pig," said my Uncle Homer.

2. "That is not an insult," I told him.

3. "Pigs are really clean animals," I said.

96

## Acronyms

An **acronym** is a word formed by the first letters of each word.

**Example:** SCUBA
**S**elf **C**ontained **U**nderwater **B**reathing **A**pparatus

**Directions:** List other acronyms you know.

| VIP | Very important person |
| DARE | Drug Abuse Resistance Education |

*Answers will vary.*

97

## Parts of a Paragraph

A **paragraph** is a group of sentences that all tell about the same thing. Most paragraphs have three parts: a **beginning**, a **middle** and an **end**.

**Directions:** Write **beginning**, **middle** or **end** next to each sentence in the scrambled paragraphs below. There can be more than one middle sentence.

**Example:**

middle — We took the tire off the car.

beginning — On the way to Aunt Louise's, we had a flat tire.

middle — We patched the hole in the tire.

end — We put the tire on and started driving again.

middle — I took all the ingredients out of the cupboard.

beginning — One morning, I decided to bake a pumpkin pie.

end — I forgot to add the pumpkin!

middle — I mixed the ingredients together, but something was missing.

middle — The sun was very hot and our throats were dry.

end — We finally decided to turn back.

beginning — We started our hike very early in the morning.

middle — It kept getting hotter as we walked.

98

### Topic Sentences

A **topic sentence** is usually the first sentence in a paragraph. It tells what the story will be about.

**Directions:** Read the following sentences. Circle the topic sentence that should go first in the paragraph that follows.

[Rainbows have seven colors.]

There's a pot of gold.

I like rainbows.

The colors are red, orange, yellow, green, blue, indigo and violet. Red forms the outer edge, with violet on the inside of the rainbow.

He cut down a cherry tree.

His wife was named Martha.

[George Washington was a good president.]

He helped our country get started. He chose intelligent leaders to help him run the country.

[Mark Twain was a great author.]

Mark Twain was unhappy sometimes.

Mark Twain was born in Missouri.

One of his most famous books is *Huckleberry Finn*. He wrote many other great books.

**99**

### Middle Sentences

**Middle sentences** support the topic sentence. They tell more about it.

**Directions:** Underline the middle sentences that support each topic sentence below.

**Topic Sentence:**

Penguins are birds that cannot fly.

Pelicans can spear fish with their sharp bills.

Many penguins waddle or hop about on land.

Even though they cannot fly, they are excellent swimmers.

Pelicans keep their food in a pouch.

**Topic Sentence:**

Volleyball is a team sport in which the players hit the ball over the net.

There are two teams with six players on each team.

My friend John would rather play tennis with Lisa.

Players can use their heads or their hands.

I broke my hand once playing handball.

**Topic Sentence:**

Pikes Peak is the most famous of all the Rocky Mountains.

Some mountains have more trees than other mountains.

Many people like to climb to the top.

Many people like to ski and camp there, too.

The weather is colder at the top of most mountains.

**100**

### Ending Sentences

**Ending sentences** are sentences that tie the story together.

**Directions:** Choose the correct ending sentence for each story from the sentences below. Write it at the end of the paragraph.

A new pair of shoes!
All the corn on the cob I could eat!
A new eraser!

#### Corn on the Cob

Corn on the cob used to be my favorite food. That is, until I lost my four front teeth. For one whole year, I had to sit and watch everyone else eat my favorite food without me. Mom gave me creamed corn, but it just wasn't the same. When my teeth finally came in, Dad said he had a surprise for me. I thought I was going to get a bike or a new C.D. player or something. I was just as happy to get what I did.

All the corn on the cob I could eat!

I would like to take a train ride every year.
Trains move faster than I thought they would.
She had brought her new gerbil along for the ride.

#### A Train Ride

When our family took its first train ride, my sister brought along a big box. She would not tell anyone what she had in it. In the middle of the trip, we heard a sound coming from the box. "Okay, Jan, now you have to open the box," said Mom. When she opened the box we were surprised.

She had brought her new gerbil along for the ride.

**101**

### Review

**Directions:** Write your own story with a topic sentence, at least three middle sentences and an ending sentence. Use your own idea or use one of these ideas for a story title:

The Best Day I Ever Had    If I Could Do Anything
My First Pet    My Best Friend
I Was So Unhappy I Cried    Why I Like Myself

Title:

_____

Topic Sentence:

_____

Middle Sentences:

_____

*Answers will vary.*

Ending Sentence:

_____

**102**

### Letter Writing

**Directions:** Write a friendly letter below. Be sure to include a heading, greeting, body, closing and signature.

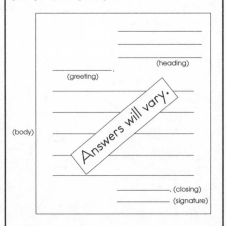

(heading)

(greeting)

(body)

*Answers will vary.*

_____ (closing)

_____ (signature)

**104**

### Poetry

**Haiku** is a form of Japanese poetry which is often about nature. There are 3 lines: 5 syllables, 7 syllables, 5 syllables.

**Example:**

The rain falls softly,    5
Touching the leaves on the trees,    7
Bathing tenderly.    5

**Directions:** Choose a topic in nature that would make a good haiku. Think of words to describe your topic. Write and illustrate your haiku below.

_____

*Answers will vary.*

**105**

# Teaching Suggestions

## Verbs

Write some action verbs, such as *run, talk, jump, watch, read, wave, drive, slide, bend,* etc, on paper. Put the pieces of paper into a hat or can. Let your child choose a sheet of paper and pantomime the word for you to guess. Take turns doing this until you've both had several turns.

## Subjects and Predicates

Give your child 20 index cards. He/she should write ten subjects on the first ten cards, and ten predicates on the remaining cards. Punch holes in the upper right hand corner of each stack and fasten with a notebook ring. Have your child flip through the stack of cards, mixing subjects and predicates to form a variety of sentences.

## Adjectives

Blindfold your child so he/she can touch, smell and hear but cannot see. Seal a scoop of ice cream in a plastic bag. Hand the bag to your child to touch without opening the bag. Ask your child to describe the ice cream using several adjectives. Write down your child's words. Repeat this activity with other objects which allow your child to describe what he/she can see, hear, smell, touch or taste.

## Compound Words

Give your child a section of the newspaper. Ask him/her to find and circle as many compound words as possible. This could also be done with other parts of speech, such as adjectives, verbs, pronouns, etc.

## Quotation Marks

From the newspaper, cut out your child's favorite comic strip. Have your child rewrite the comic strip conversations, using sentences with quotation marks. Check your child's sentences for proper use of quotation marks and discuss what you find with your child.

## Antonyms

Have your child write a list of antonym word pairs, such as *light, dark; silent, noisy; neat, sloppy;* etc. Encourage him/her to use a variety of words. The list should contain about 10–12 word pairs. With this list, help your child make an Antonym Tree. Have on hand scissors, glue, some colored markers or crayons and several sheets of construction paper of different sizes and colors. Have your child cut out a tree trunk and branches and glue them onto a large white background paper. Cut out leaves of various colors. Your child can then print the antonym pairs on the different leaves and glue them onto the tree branches. Synonym or homophone pairs could also be used.

# Antonyms, Synonyms and Homophones

From construction paper, cut out 30 carrots, 30 beets and 30 potatoes. Write 15 pairs of homophones on the carrots, 15 pairs of antonyms on the beets and 15 pairs of synonyms on the potatoes, one word per card. Have your child match the pairs. On the back of each pair, write an identical mark, letter or number so that your child can check his/her responses independently.

## Journals

Encourage your child to write in a daily journal. Provide a spiral notebook with wide-spaced lines. Journal entries are usually anecdotal and personal. Encourage your child to ask questions, describe dreams or write accounts of his/her day in the journal. Following are some suggestions for journal starters:

I'd like to go . . .                  I want to know more about . . .
My birthday is . . .                 Did you know . . .
Sometimes I feel . . .               My favorite . . .
I laughed and laughed . . .          My best friend is . . .
I went to . . .                      When I got to the party . . .
I felt silly . . .                   Was I ever mad when . . .
I really miss . . .                  I feel _____ when . . .
I try hard to . . .                  Last night when I went to bed . . .
I can't wait until . . .             I felt so proud when . . .

## Poetry

Encourage your child to compose poems, copying the patterns of the following poetry:

Couplet (a two-line rhyme)

**Example:**    I saw a cloud way up high
                Soaring gently in the sky.

Limerick (a humorous poem that has the end rhyme scheme of AABBA)

**Example:**    There was a young man from Maine (A)
                Who liked to stand out in the rain (A)
                Although he's all wet, (B)
                He's standing there yet. (B)
                That crazy young man from Maine. (A)

Quatrain (a four-line poem with end rhymes of AABB or ABAB)

**Examples:**   AABB                          ABAB
                I asked a small boy (A)        As I watched a waterfall, (A)
                Who played with a toy (A)      Water splashed upon my face. (B)
                Why trees do not rain. (B)     Although I was quite small, (A)
                He could not explain. (B)      I knew it was a grand place. (B)